WORLD CUP'78

■ THE ■
GAME
OF THE
CENTURY

Fontana Original

WORLD CUP '78

▪THE▪ GAME OF THE CENTURY

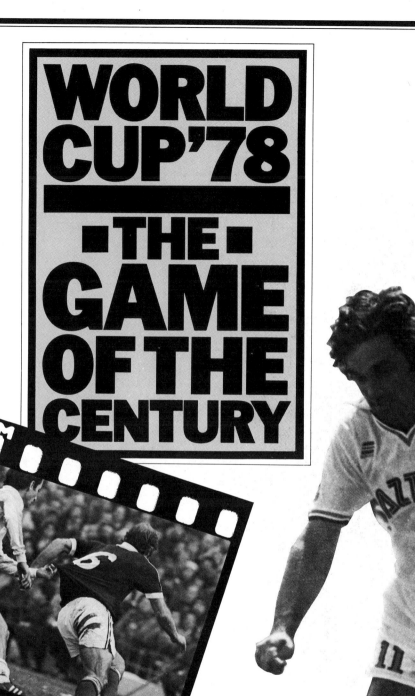

Derek Conrad▪Robert Sidaway▪Bob Wilson

Derek Conrad first entered the film industry in 1952. He worked as a floor manager and cameraman before producing and directing films, documentaries, shorts and commercials; to date he has won eleven international awards for these. His experience ranges from Hammer horror and television advertising to ambitious international projects like **Game of the Century.** He has also written scripts and screenplays and worked on magazines like **Films and Filming** and **Plays and Players.**

Robert Sidaway was born in 1942. An avid follower of football, with a penchant for his home team Wolverhampton Wanderers, he studied at the London Academy of Music and Dramatic Art. As a professional actor he appeared in productions in the West End and in the United States and Canada as well as on television. He subsequently moved into drama production and writing. He lives in Brighton with his son Ashley and dreams of international honours on the football field.

Bob Wilson was born in Chesterfield, Derbyshire, in 1941. He was educated at Chesterfield Grammar School and Loughborough College and taught for a while in London before joining Arsenal FC in 1964. He made over 300 first team appearances in goal for them, winning FA Cup, League Championship and Fairs Cup medals. He had previously represented England at Under-15 and amateur levels and – qualifying on parentage – has represented Scotland as a full international. Since his retirement in 1974 he has worked as a sports commentator for the BBC and in the press. He is married with three children and lives in Hertfordshire.

The authors wish to thank the following
for their invaluable help and advice:

Sir Stanely Rous, CBE
Jack Rollin
Ken Aston
Jack Taylor
Ashley Sidaway
Fédération Internationale de Football Association (FIFA)

First published in Fontana 1978
Copyright © Derek Conrad, Robert Sidaway, Bob Wilson 1978

Book and cover design by Ken Carroll

Made and printed in Great Britain by
William Collins Sons & Co Ltd, Glasgow

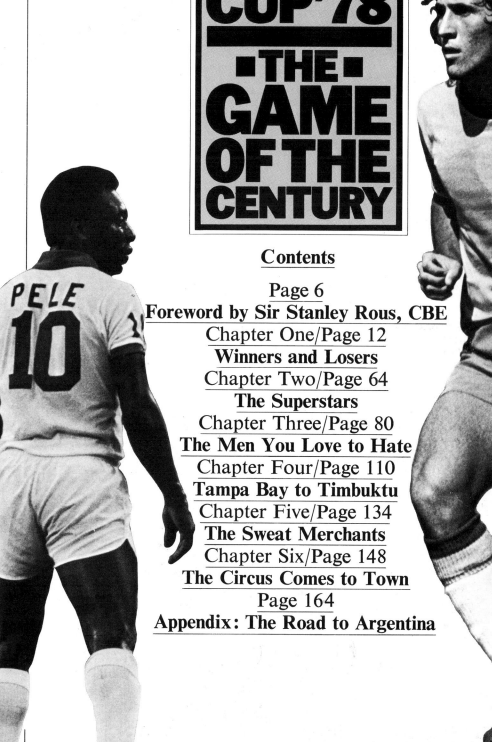

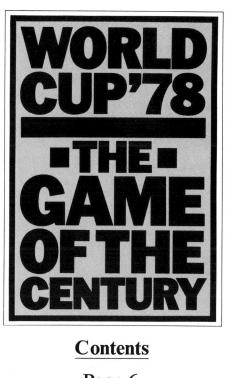

WORLD CUP'78

∎THE∎ GAME OF THE CENTURY

Contents

FOREWORD BY
SIR STANLEY ROUS, CBE

Many books have been written about association football, but this one is different. It is intended to serve two purposes, one as a companion for the film of the same title which will give readers a pre-1978 World Cup review, showing how players, managers, referees, organisers, administrators, superstars and back-room boys help to produce a festival of football every four years and, secondly, to provide a very readable account of the development of the game throughout the world during the twentieth century.

The eyes and ears of the whole football world will be directed towards Argentina in June 1978, but many followers will be interested to read before this time of the increasing work which goes on for the three years before the final event. Two World Cup organising committees and numerous sub-committees are formed within FIFA and the host country whose work is to cover every aspect of the world's biggest one-sport event, which is second only to the Olympic Games in world-wide scale. Television will play a large part in the World Cup organisation: in the last World Cup final in 1974 in the Federal Republic of Germany it is estimated that an audience of more than 1000 million was attracted to the screen.

The pattern of the World Cup organisation, as outlined in this book, will be similar in 1982 in Spain and 1986 in Colombia, and the work and responsibilities of FIFA and the host country identical, so that the reader will be informed of future policies and procedures. They may vary, though, if the proposal of President Havelange for 24 teams to compete in the final round is adopted. European football associations have so far rejected the increased number. They feel that in the final round, the strongest football nations should compete and the game should not be a contest between the most successful teams from each of the continental confederations.

During my presidency I submitted a memorandum to the FIFA World Cup Organising Committee outlining five different formula for the final competition – for 32, 24, 16, 12 and 8 teams – showing the number of sub-seats required and the number of matches and length of each tournament. When the last sixteen are known I would favour another round of home and away matches (all sixteen in a straight draw) and the eight winners meeting in the final tournament which would require much less time for completion and rule out matches of little interest between teams in a neutral country.

After Colombia 1986, however, unless one country is prepared to bear the cost of organising the final competition, groups of countries such as the Benelux (Holland, Belgium, Luxembourg) or the Central European area (Yugoslavia, Austria, Hungary and Czechoslovakia), with a sub-seat in each capital city, may apply to stage the final round.

Those schemes are for future considerations. The immediate problem is Argentina 1978, to which country I went in 1964 at the invitation of the Argentinian Football Association to explore the

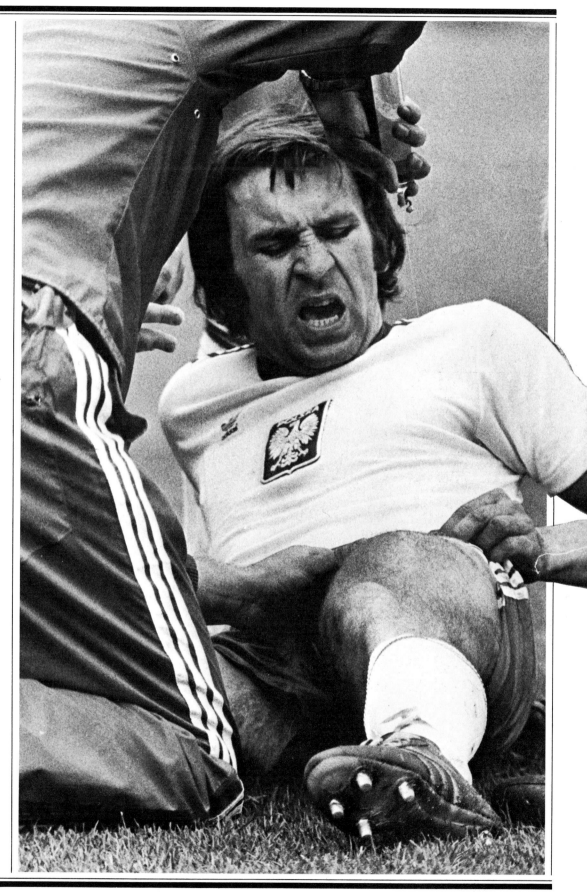

possibilities of a World Cup being staged there.
I met the president of the country, saw the existing stadiums and was taken to cities suggested as sub-seats. I was quickly made aware of the immense interest and enthusiasm for football when attending matches in Buenos Aires, Rosario and Cordoba. From that time, thirteen years ago, I have felt certain that the Argentinian government and football authorities, in spite of trials and tribulations in the meantime, would not let this opportunity slip away.

This book tells the story of all that is involved in staging a World Cup. It invites experts Ken Aston and Jack Taylor to tell the referee's side of the story, lets players like Beckenbauer and Cruyff talk about their hopes and fears, allows officials of FIFA to explain their part in the immense operation. There are chapters, too, outlining the great progress made recently in football in the developing countries and explaining their ambition to play a bigger part in the World Cup. Their sporting prestige is a great concern to them.
I hope the book will be widely read before, during and after the successive World Cup tournaments, wherever they are staged.

Sir Stanley Rous London March 1978

Chapter One

WINNERS AND LOSERS

The World Cup has become the single most prized trophy in sporting history and June 1978 will see 16 nations competing in Argentina for the Golden Statuette and all the glory that is attached to it.

From the moment in Munich in 1974 when Franz Beckenbauer held the FIFA World Cup high – the symbolic victory salute to audiences around the world after West Germany had beaten Holland in the final – soccer has been preparing itself for the 1978 Finals. Nearly two billion people will watch the victories and defeats, the joy and despair, in the battle for gold. The modern game will come under the powerful microscope of the media; its sheer force and vitality, its urgency, cruelty, subtlety and skill will be exhaustively analysed. Bouquets and brickbats will be thrown at the superstars, the superteams and their motivators. But whatever triumphs and disasters are spotlighted in the supercharged atmosphere of Argentina, this eleventh World Cup tournament will prove – if proof were needed – that football on this level sets the adrenalin of all nations racing. It is indisputably the game of the century.

The Beginnings

What is football? It is said to be the madness of the English, for in the beginning the game was developed exclusively by the English. England was the cradle of the modern game, and in 1863, when the Football Association was formed, the basics for the game that was to spread world-wide were born. It must be made clear that when we talk of 'the basics of the game' we mean the modern game. There are solid indications that football, in one form or another, was played over two thousand years ago among the Chinese of the Han Dynasty. It was played as part of their military training, to encourage comradeship and discipline. The most striking feature of this game was the fact that the severed head of an enemy warrior was used as the ball!

A less grisly version of the game, which dates back to the early sixteenth century, can still be seen today. This is an annual re-enactment of two games of *calcio*, played on summer feast days in the Piazza della Signoria in Florence between two teams of twenty-seven colourfully dressed players in Renaissance costumes. However, in general the early history of

Below: Association Football game, 1888.
Facing page top: Scotland's Renton FC, the first World Champions in 1887-8. They challenged – and beat – Preston North End and West Bromwich Albion to earn this rather exaggerated title. They claimed to derive their strength from drinking chicken bree.
Facing page below: English international team, 1890.
Facing page far right: The captain of the Lady Football Players, about 1895. At this period, there were many women's teams in England, an example being the famous Amazons football team. Recent years have seen a revival of women's football internationally.

FOULKE — THE SHEFFIELD GOAL KEEPER

TAKING A KICK

International Football Match. 8 March. 1873.

Balance Sheet.

To Gate Money	99.12.0	By Ground, Expenses (Gate, &c.)	2.0.0
To Tickets	6.9.0	" Loan of Tent	1.0.0
		" Putting up &c.	.12.6
		" Bill Sticker	1.5.
		" Printing Bills	.10.6
		" do Cards	
		" Use of Ground	10.0.0
		" Dinners to Scotch 11	13.2.0
		" Ball	12.6
		" Luncheons to Scotch	2.12.6
		" Police	17.6
			73.8

'An early form of football, played in China over 2000 years ago, used the severed head of an enemy warrior as the ball'

the game was hard and bloody, and every civilized culture since the Han Dynasty has left relics in word, painting and sculpture of 'a football game'. Normans, Romans, royalists, peasants, heathens and knaves, sailors and armies, all indulged in and then spread the game of football throughout the world.

'A bloody and murthering practice rather than a felowly sport or pastime' is the manner in which football was described by the puritans in early eighteenth-century England. Football then was played to undefined rules by any number of people, and one game could stretch for any length of time, in fields, parks or main highways. Matches could become very violent: four centuries earlier, Edward II had banned football in London on pain of imprisonment because of the 'great noise in the city caused by hustling over large balls, from which many evils may arise'. Travelling further back in time to AD 217, one discovers that on Shrove Tuesday at Ashbourne in Derbyshire a ferocious game was played by two teams – two halves of the same town – across the countryside. In fact, it is still played today. This type of game was common across England and was normally played on high days and holidays. A Frenchman visiting England in the mid-eighteenth century who saw such a 'sporting pastime' on a public holiday remarked that 'if the Englishmen call this "playing" it would be impossible to say what they would call "fighting".'

As in England, so across the world nations were playing their own versions of football. Egyptians, Assyrians and Greeks, all had sown the seed for the modern game. In ancient Mexico the skill of heading and kicking balls through silk screens or rings set high in a wall was much appreciated, whilst the delicate skill and acrobatic artistry of a gentle game in Burma, still played today, where teams of men kicked a wicker-work ball about without it ever stopping or touching the ground, is breathtaking to watch.

Kemari is an ancient form of Japanese football. It was introduced into Japan around the fifth century, when Buddhism found its way into the country and Japanese culture was flowering. It was at first played exclusively at court and by the aristocracy, gradually gaining popularity with the masses. Before *kemari* begins there is the *eda-mari* ceremony, and a game of *komari*. *Eda-mari* is a ball attached to a branch from an evergreen which is offered before the Deity. The

Facing page top: Association Football Cup Final, 1902, between Sheffield United and Southampton. The 1-1 draw was watched by 74,479 spectators.

Facing page below: Balance sheet from an international game between England and Scotland in 1873. The first ever international between these countries was played the year before, ending in a diplomatic goal-less draw.

Below: The earliest known photograph of a football team – Addiscombe Military College, 1855.

7th' June 1901.

Sir,

I have the honour to inform you that I have submitted to The King your letter of the 16th' Inst: and in reply I am commanded to say that His Majesty is pleased to accede to the request contained in it ,to grant his Patronage to The Football Association.

I am Sir,

Your obedient Servant,

General.

Keeper of H. M's Privy Purse.

Association.

Standing (from left to right): J. W. Carter. John Lewis. W. H. Haskins. F. Styles. J. Albert. Nat Whittaker. Kemp. S. A. Notcutt. N. Malcolmson. W. J. Wilson.

[Photo by kind permission of the Football Association.] [The Book of Football Copyright]

Sitting (on left of table): R. P. Gregson. McKenna. R. E. Lythgoe. D. B. Woolfall. F. J. Wall. J. C. Clegg. C. Crump. C. S. Sherrington. C. J. Hughes. J. J. Bentley.

Sitting (on right of table): W. H. Bellamy. H. S. Radford. A. G. Hines. A. Kingscott. M. T. Roberts. W. Pickford. Alfred Davis. W. McGregor. G. W. Simmons.

'A bloody and murthering practice rather than a felowly sport or pastime'

elder receiving this offering walks slowly and gracefully to *mari-tsubo*, the playing field, takes the ball from the branch and then produces it magically from under the sleeve of his ceremonial costume. This creates great excitement amongst the spectators, and the elder has to perfect this trick over many years! Following the ceremony, eight players enter the field to play *komari*. The field is divided into eight parts, called *hakkyo* or 'eight boundaries'.

The best player takes the No. 1 position and kicks the ball below shoulder height to each player. The ball is then kicked in a clockwise direction.

When *komari* is over, the traditional *kemari* begins. Nobody wins or loses: the game is played in deep friendship, the players united in mental attitude to enjoy the game and entertain the crowd. Each player

Facing page top: Royal recognition of the Football Association, nearly 40 years after the FA first began to seek such an honour and thus gain respectability for the game – something which it had not always enjoyed in the past. Nowadays Royalty is often present at important games in Britain.
Facing page below: The general enquiry office of the Football Association in High Holborn, London, about 1905.
Above: The FA Council in session in the early years of the century.

tries to beat the other by swift passing and bouncing the ball to great heights. It's an amazing sight to see players congratulating each other over the fifteen to twenty minutes' playing time. The players wear uniforms signifying rank and splashed with rich colours, fine examples of Japanese costume and culture.

The basic belief of the game is that the higher the football bounces, the nearer to their god they become.

Kings, puritans, dictators, all tried to stamp out a pastime that nobody invented. Wherever combatants were trying to force a round object through other combatants' territory to reach a specific target, the game that would eventually develop into modern football was flowering. It continued to flower, and by the start of the 1800s was on the threshold of the modern game we know today.

At this time in England, the rough-and-tumble game played by the working class was being encouraged as a spectator sport by the gentry. They did not actually play themselves and give the game the aristocratic backing that cricket was enjoying, but they did turn out to watch and enjoy the spirit of a game played by the lower classes. At this time, private education for the privileged was developing very quickly; the public school came into being and establishments such as Eton, Harrow, Charterhouse, Rugby and Winchester were fast developing varying footballing games for scholars thirsting for some form of organized sporting pastime. The most famous version of such a footballing game is the Eton Wall Game, still played each year on St Andrew's Day. Twenty players form each side on a pitch 120 yards long by 6 yards wide, with the goals at each end being a tree and a garden door. In this century, only two goals have ever been scored!

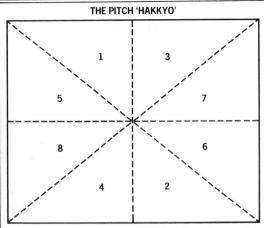

THE PITCH 'HAKKYO'

```
        1           3

   5                    7



   8                    6

        4           2
```

While at public school, it was fine for a boy to play a game with rules, a great improvement on the football being played by apprentices and peasants, but what happened when a young man left school and entered university or started a profession in a city and wished to continue playing his version of football? Problems were bound to, and did, exist until 1848, when fourteen representatives of the public schools, led by Eton, Harrow and Winchester, presented themselves at Cambridge to develop a universal set of rules acceptable to all establishments. In consequence, the so-called 'Cambridge Rules' came about, which were to be adapted and changed twice by 1860.

Competition was now a possibility for schools and universities alike. Scholars and students were able to play a game established on a common foundation. The now legendary inter-school and inter-university matches commenced and played to rules such as: 'a goal to be awarded when the ball is kicked between two flag posts and under the string'; 'Catching the ball to be allowed as long as it is directly from the foot and the catcher must not run with it but kick it immediately'; 'Throw-ins to be taken with only one hand'. Even an offside rule was introduced.

At this time, when the scholastic brains of the south were busy shaping the game, a collection of cricketers and friends from the Collingswood School were setting up a football club in Sheffield. They developed rules that were very similar to, though a little rougher than, the Cambridge Rules. One important and sensible rule stated that every playing member of the club should have two caps, one red and one blue, to distinguish the teams whilst playing among themselves. By 1860 there were fifteen football clubs in Sheffield.

For the next three years, the so-called law-makers were hammering out rules and regulations far too regularly. They were published, withdrawn, revised,

Right: On the way to the FA Cup Final, 1907.
Facing page top: Sir Frederick Wall, Secretary of the FA from 1895 to 1934. His suspicions of international football kept England out of the World Cup until 1950.
Facing page below: Press advertisement for a lethal football boot, about 1900. Modern defenders take note.
Following pages: The 1911 FA Cup Final in progress at Crystal Palace. Bradford City beat Newcastle United after a replay. Key games are now a major spectacle.

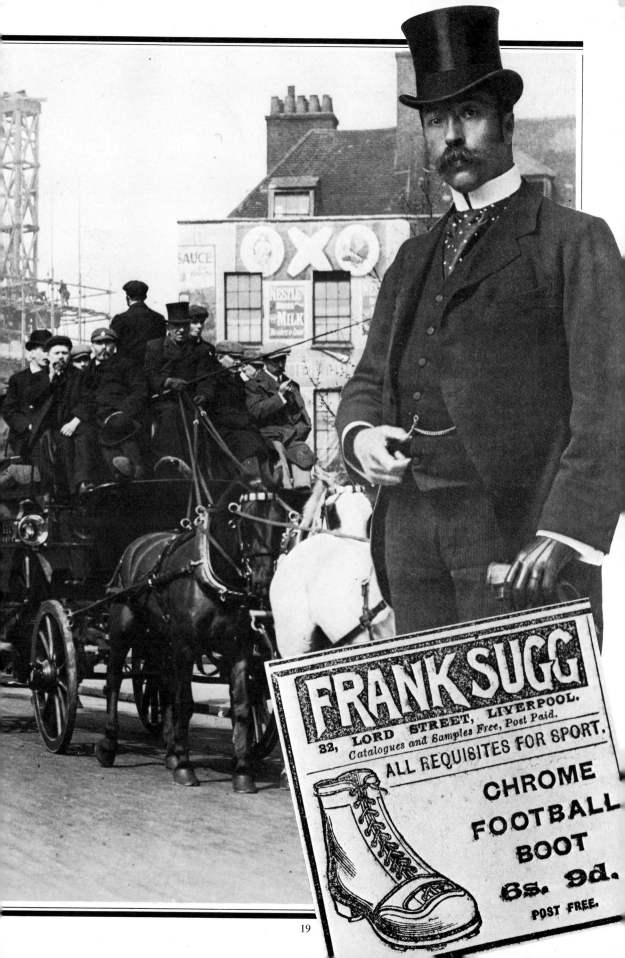

renegotiated and re-published to the confusion of clubs springing up throughout the country. Players must have wondered what version of the game they were to play from match to match! However, down-to-earth commonsense prevailed. At Uppingham School in Rutland, where they had already introduced a crossbar rather than tapes, the renowned Victorian educationalist, J. C. Thring, penned a set of rules entitled 'The Simplest Game'. Here were straight-forward rules – no kicking at the ball in the air, no player allowed in front of the ball and most important, no violence whatsoever. New thoughts developed at Cambridge again. In 1862, in a match between Cambridge Old Harrovians and Cambridge Old Etonians, it was ruled that there should be eleven players on each side, a neutral referee and two umpires (one from each side), a three-man offside rule and goalposts 20ft high by 12ft across. Thring's rules, and the new Cambridge rules, worked quite well and were to form the main part of the thinking of the Football Association which was only a few months away from being formed.

Coming of Age

In October 1863 football came of age, and the true foundations of the modern game were laid in a London public house, the Freemasons Arms, by a body which called itself the Football Association. From this moment on, through much bitterness and at times fury, the game passed from the schools and universities to the clubs. From the time of this meeting until the turn of the century, the game took its definitive shape.

Running with the ball was soon dropped and a player was not allowed to 'hack' – meaning to kick a man on the shin when dribbling. Out went 'making a mark', achieved by catching the ball, marking the spot with the boot and therefore winning a free kick. Out, quite quickly, went an original FA rule of 'touch-down'; this was allowing a free kick at goal after the ball had been kicked or carried over a goal line and touched down by an attacking player. Offside, though, continued to cause considerable argument. The FA's early directive was 'no one interfering with play in front of the ball'. It is obvious how much of the essence of rugby football as we know it is in these rejected rules. In fact, it was not long before the 'manly and courageous' gentlemen, who favoured 'marking', 'touch-down' and carrying the ball, called the dribbling-men 'absolute cowards' and walked out of the FA to form their own associa-tion, linking strongly with the universities, and identi-fying their game as rugby football.

Now minds of one accord could get on with developing football. Very soon, only the goalkeeper could handle the ball, and attacking play came into force by allowing forward passing of the ball, making football much more exciting to watch. In 1872, nine years after the London pub meeting, the first ever official international match was played. It was between England and Scotland. A most diplomatic result was achieved – a 0-0 draw.

In 1871 the FA Cup began its famous history. In 1878, referees were first allowed to use whistles. Rigid goal cross-bars were made compulsory in 1882, and

> **Catching the ball to be allowed as long as it is directly from the foot and the catcher must not run with it but kick it immediately**
>
> Cambridge Rules, 1848

to go with them, goal nets and linesmen in 1891. That same year, penalty kicks were allowed for the first time. The 'honourable game of football' was fast becoming the most popular team sporting pursuit that Great Britain and subsequently the world was to know.

From now on, the game spread rapidly abroad. British businessmen, soldiers, sailors, and engineers introduced the game to Europe and South America. By 1889, Holland and Denmark had founded their own football associations. In 1892 Argentina became the first country outside Britain to inaugurate a national championship. At the same time football was being played in Austria and at the turn of the century the game had reached Germany, Hungary and Uruguay, where national football associations were founded.

Football became one of Britain's greatest exports. Even in Russia, two Englishmen launched the game through their cotton mill in Orekhovo Zuyero. In Chile and Uruguay there are still clubs named Everton and Liverpool, so called after the sailors who played matches against the locals when their ships were in dock. In the USA the universities, once again, were the first disciples and the names of early clubs such as Kensington FC of Saint Louis and Shamrock FC of Cincinnati indicated their British origin.

Children in grimy back alleys in the north of England or on soft sand in South America were now playing a universal game; football had travelled far. However, although the British were undisputed leaders in the field of football legislation – a British team had in fact toured Germany and Czechoslovakia, and the country had played hosts in 1900 to a team from Brussels – they declined to take part in the organising of football internationals. Just when Europe looked to them to establish a world governing body, the FA cold-shouldered the idea. It was left to the French to implant the idea of international competition, the springboard that would eventually bring about the World Cup.

Birth of the World Cup

Four now legendary gentlemen, Robert Guerin, a lawyer, C. A. W. Hirschman, a Dutch banker, Henri Delaunay, a printer and Jules Rimet, a publisher, called a meeting in Paris on 21 May, 1904.

These men, excited by the upsurge in the popularity of the game and seeing the potential of soccer as a world sport, decided to organise a world championship. They grandly called themselves the *Federation Internationale de Football Association*, or as the organisation is more generally known today, FIFA. These pioneering French gentlemen were joined at that summer meeting by representatives from Sweden, Switzerland, Spain, Denmark, Belgium and the Netherlands. A World Cup would not be contested, though, for another 26 years.

However, Jules Rimet, whose name belongs to the original World Cup statuette, and Henri Delaunay worked slavishly over the years to bring about their cherished dream. Rimet loved the game dearly and was a great and charming diplomat. His record as President of the French Football Federation from 1919 to 1949 and President of FIFA from 1921 to 1954, not long before his death, was a rather special achievement. Delaunay, his counterpart, was a tireless worker, full of the vision of a world championship and determined to see it realised. FIFA's seven founder members started the laborious task of linking the various national federations into one organisation to co-ordinate the game throughout Europe, and as one proud clause stated in the statutes of the first meeting, *FIFA has the sole right to organise a World Championship.*

A world championship must have seemed a viable proposition which could be swiftly brought about, as the Olympic Games in 1900 and 1904 had launched a football competition. However, much time and patience was required to bring about the first World Cup in 1930. By 1914 there were twenty-four members including England, who had joined in 1905 and had D. B. Woolfall, a member of the Football Association, made President of FIFA in 1906. FIFA's yardstick for law-making was measured against England's own International Board which was formed for the express purpose of drawing up and carrying out the laws of the game. FIFA gained representation on this board in 1913. Germany, Italy, Czechoslovakia, Hungary and Finland were now present and FIFA was starting to become a very powerful body.

That power was to be drained away during the 1914–18 War. The work and ideals of FIFA were halted whilst the bigger game of war was played. Obviously the idea of international football was shattered; FIFA's ideals lay in shreds and it was to take the organisation a full 15 years to recover and regain many of its former members.

When the war ended FIFA had to cope with bitter reactions. England, Scotland, Ireland, Wales, Belgium, Luxembourg and France herself decided to boycott Germany and her allies in the Association. Eventually, England and the other three home countries left FIFA in 1920, which unfortunately ended FIFA's representation on the International Board. Nevertheless, slowly but surely FIFA began to resurrect its ideals. Jules Rimet was firmly in the driving seat now, and in 1921, at the age of 48, he became President, a term

Below: FIFA's original headquarters in Zurich, and the first World Cup trophy, later named after Jules Rimet in honour of his central role in developing the World Cup championship. It was given to Brazil to keep in perpetuity in 1970.

of office which was to last 33 years. The Olympic Games Football Finals in 1924 were a success and this boded well for a stronger FIFA. England returned and so did many of the original members. In 1928 international football was further strengthened in the Olympics of that year and FIFA campaigned for all the competing footballers to be paid to compensate for loss of earnings. The International Olympic Committee grudgingly accepted this, though it was against their sporting principles. England was not prepared to see the game pushed into a financially competitive arena and left FIFA again, not to return this time for more than eighteen years.

At this time the South American Football Federation was formed and the Republic of Uruguay was pioneering this Continent's football. The 1928 Olympics saw the Uruguayans win the football competition as they had done in 1924. Rimet, with superb timing and showmanship after the 2-1 victory over Argentina, interested the President of Uruguay in hosting the first tournament. As one Uruguayan politician said: 'Other nations have their history, we have our football.' 1930 also marked the centenary of Uruguay's independence and the first World Cup took place in Montevideo. Rimet and Delaunay were at last to see their dream fulfilled.

1930: The Long Trek

Tiny Uruguay, proud of its footballing prowess, amazingly offered to foot every bill for this first World Cup, including travelling and hotel expenses for all the visiting teams. They decided to build a brand new stadium for the tournament. It was erected in Montevideo and appropriately named the Centenary Stadium. Incredibly it was built in only eight months and they had the rainy season to compete with in that period! The stadium stood at the end of 18 July Avenue, and staged its first game appropriately enough on that same date – 1930 –

'Other nations have their history, we have our football'

Uruguay playing Peru and winning 1-0 in front of a delirious Uruguayan crowd.

However, for Uruguay and FIFA there were only 13 entrants for this first world tournament. FIFA was disappointed and the Latin American federations were embittered and insulted, mainly because of the few European entries. Two months before the kick-off there were no European countries likely to be present at all. Eventually, Belgium, Romania, France and Yugoslavia (not exactly the élite of the European footballing nations) joined with Argentina, Chile, Mexico, Brazil, Bolivia, Peru, Paraguay and the USA to present themselves in Uruguay. No direct airline travel was available, so the gruelling journey for the Europeans was to take 14 days by boat. Officials and players were to be away at least ten weeks. King Carol of Romania proudly hand-picked his country's team himself. He had always been known as a promoter of sport in his country. When he first came to the throne, he had granted an amnesty to all Romanian footballers. He also brought pressure to bear on various companies

Below left: Stabile (arm raised) nets Argentina's first goal in the 1930 final against Uruguay.
Below right: The 1930 Argentinian team.
Facing page top: Painting by W. H. Overend of a match in progress in 1890. Note heavy boots.
Facing page below: Jules Rimet at the time of his appointment as President of the French Football Federation in 1919, a decade away from the first World Cup.

24

employing players for time off with pay – another feather in FIFA's cap towards professionalism. France was gently pressurised into going by Rimet, and R. W. Seeldrayers, FIFA's veteran Vice-President, persuaded his Belgian Association to send a team. Yugoslavia eventually conceded to the call. The French, Romanians and Belgians travelled on the same boat, picking up the Brazilians en route; the Yugoslavian team had sailed two days earlier. On arrival, the European teams and their entourage were given a tumultuous welcome. Their participation was greatly appreciated and was to be justly remembered, although their standard of play was soon to be forgotten.

But the standard of football within the Uruguayan, Argentinian, American and Brazilian ranks was high. Uruguay were clear favourites with excessive talent and home advantage, though the Argentinians were expected to prove traditional, tough and attacking opponents. Brazil were the exciting Latin unknowns and the USA, in the main British with five Scots and an Englishman, were looked on to show strength and enterprise in their tiny shorts worn over strapping legs! The American players were so strongly built that they earned the nickname 'The Shot-Putters'. The final became a repeat of the 1928 Olympic Final: the traditional enemies, Uruguay and Argentina, were to face each other. In Buenos Aires the atmosphere was electric and fans were swarming like ants on to the chartered packet-boats which carried them across the River Plate. As they left, fireworks lit the night sky and chants of 'victory or death' rang out. Maximum security was required: soldiers circled the Centenary Stadium, the crowd was limited to 90,000 and as many as possible were searched for revolvers. Fixed bayonets kept the crowds outside moving and the referee, in cap and plus-fours, was given a body-guard. Waves of excitement ebbed and flowed in and around the stadium. It was to be a fine and dramatic match which even had a major confrontation before the kick-off, with both teams insisting on playing with their own ball. Argentina won the toss for it, but Uruguay took the final 4-2.

The game had been good-tempered and so had the

> # Soldiers circled the stadium, the crowd was limited to 90,000 and as many as possible were searched for revolvers. Fixed bayonets kept the crowds outside moving and the referee was given a bodyguard

banner-waving crowd. The following day was declared a national holiday in Uruguay, the flags flew high, and the ship's sirens sounded in the port. In Argentina, however, a mob stoned the Uruguayan consulate and police had to fire on a hostile crowd.

Jules Rimet had the Golden Cup, designed by the French sculptor Abel Lafleur and costing 50,000 francs, presented to the jubilant Uruguayan team. FIFA must have felt satisfied and perhaps not a little relieved, for the first World Cup Tournament, against the odds, had been launched with considerable success.

1934: A Political Triumph

The 1934 tournament was a highly competitive one. Thirty-two nations entered and sixteen made the finals in Italy. For the only time in World Cup history the holders, Uruguay, did not defend their title. They were still embittered by the defection of the Europeans in 1930 and they were also suffering from one of their occasional players' strikes. Italy planned the tournament thoroughly; they were determined to win and duly did so. With the eyes of the world focused on his country, Mussolini cleverly turned the event into one enormous advertisement for his fascist party, as Hitler was to do with the Nuremburg Olympics two years later. Mussolini's team, the

Azzurri (Blues), were in the care of Vittorio Pozzo, a great believer in the tactics and approach of the English to their football. He also created a great atmosphere of discipline and gritty determination among his team, an obvious echo of the fascist climate of the times. Pozzo called himself 'king, with a strong hand'. He had to be to deal with his talented and highly temperamental players.

FIFA had granted Italy the final at the Stockholm Congress of 1932. It was obvious now that only countries with large resources could stage the finals, for the scale of the tournament was growing. Little Uruguay had managed to foot the bill in 1930 and make a satisfactory profit, but it is doubtful that they could have sustained the 1934 costs. The Italian federation promised that they were 'capable of sustaining these burdens even in the case of an adverse balance . . . using the numerous and flourishing Italian cities, all provided with magnificent stadiums'. On Mussolini's orders, the fascist government was determined to pick up the costs. The favourites for the final were Italy and the Austrian 'Wonderteam', even though it was past its peak. Austria was managed by Hugo Meisl, another advocate of English football. Meisl was a great friend of Herbert Chapman, the

Previous pages: Painting by an unknown artist of an English football match, about 1850.
Facing page: FIFA official posters for the first four World Cup tournaments. Their high artistic quality reflects not only FIFA's attention to details like these but also the importance of the games across the world.
Above: Vittorio Pozzo and his victorious Italian side in 1934. Political pressures are forgotten as he is chaired by his jubilant players after the final whistle.

Yorkshireman who developed Arsenal FC. Pozzo had also admired and been linked with Manchester United.

Out of the 32 teams entered for the qualifying tournament, 22 were European; one team came from Africa and one from Asia, plus eight from the Americas. Britain was not represented. The United States were again present and these strapping gentlemen were soundly thrashed by Italy 7-1. The Brazilians with their glittering talent went out hastily to Spain 3-1; their period of glory was still to come. Little Sweden disposed of Argentina 3-2, Czechoslovakia marched steadily on and so did the talented Italians. Mussolini was continually present at the German and Italian matches, proud, upright, heavy-chinned and always sporting his yachting cap. The expected final between Italy and Austria became the semi-final in Milan. To the fascist government's delight Italy triumphed 1-0. In the other semi-final Germany failed against Czechoslovakia 3-1; Mussolini showed a restrained and neutral appearance.

Apart from the many Czechs already in Rome, hundreds travelled by special trains and cars across the Alps. Parcels of gifts and souvenirs arrived for the Czech team, including 1700 telegrams. The support was insufficient. The final was resolved after extra time, Italy emerging victorious by two goals to one. However, the Czech team returned to Prague national heroes. Twenty thousand greeted them at the railway station and a civic reception was held. The republican state presented the players with gold medals.

For the Italians it was a victory they had made theirs even before the tournament commenced. More gold medals were distributed at Mussolini's team reception, the golden statuette was on display and a

Above: Four years later, Italy again win the World Cup in Paris. Pozzo holds the trophy aloft.

rumoured 10,000 lire was given to each player. Italy had profited materially and politically and whatever reservations FIFA may have had over the political implications, the World Cup and all it involved was now becoming a hot commercial property.

1938: Success amidst Turmoil

By 1938, the war clouds were gathering and Europe was in turmoil. However, there were 36 entries this time. Austria had to withdraw when they were invaded and annexed by Germany and to add insult, the Germans snatched Austria's best players. Spain was in the midst of civil war. Uruguay was again absent, for the finals were once more in Europe, and Argentina refused to compete, for they had wanted to stage this tournament themselves. Their refusal had caused riots in Buenos Aires, which the police had to stamp out. The new *Azzurri* were marching to France, determined to retain gold.

This World Cup was a Parisian spectacular and the richest footballing circus yet. Two million francs were spent on the teams' accommodation and travelling expenses. Millions more went in organization and allowances, and as the games closed some one and a half million francs were distributed between the competing associations after FIFA had received their 10% cut. This tournament was a triumph in organization, and contained some spectacular, if at times violent, football.

Italy nearly tasted defeat in the first round by the Norwegians. The crowds in Marseilles were shocked at Italy's fascist salute on the pitch before the game commenced. The anti-fascist spectators were enraged and hurled insults at Pozzo's men. Pozzo in his usual disciplinarian mood made the *Azzurri* hold the salute until the crowd quietened, and then once more the players raised their arms. A victory was gained by Italy before the ball was kicked but the players must have felt extremely tense about the whole business. The Norwegians then proceeded to make them even more nervous. Italy won their hardest match only after extra time, 2-1.

Brazil showed in this competition that its earth was becoming as rich in footballers as it was in emeralds or topaz, Poland going down 6-5 to them. The Czechs were next to go out in a replay against the exciting Brazilian talent. The first game was one of violence; two Czechs were lost to the game, one with a broken leg and the goalkeeper with a broken arm. Another was sent off along with two Brazilians. Germany, with four Austrian players, left early, Switzerland managing a replay win 4-2. Hungary and Sweden managed high-scoring victories, 6-0 against the Dutch East Indies and 8-0 against Cuba respectively. This tournament included Cuba and the Dutch East Indies for the first and only time in World Cup history.

The semi-finals saw little Sweden – now called 'the team of steel' – matched with Hungary. Although this day was the eightieth birthday of Sweden's

monarch, Gustav V, it was of no help: they were crushed 5-1. 'An excellent training match for the Hungarians,' a French player was heard to remark.

France had left the competition in the second round at the hands of Italy, 3-1. Italy faced the skilful and instinctive Brazilians in their semi-final and triumphed 2-1. The ever-modest Pozzo was quoted by the press as saying: 'I am no magician – I content myself with guiding the players with good sense. Their conscience and discipline does the rest.' It did. Italy deservedly won a fine final against Hungary 4-2. The only shadow over the game was the Hungarian press's reaction to the team selection and their manager, Dietz, was forced to resign.

The finals had pushed the war clouds away for fifteen days. FIFA had, at home, shown that the World Cup tournament was a truly worthwhile exercise and, in terms of hard cash and sport, the French finals were a success.

Twelve Empty Years

Now came a long pause. Although three countries – Brazil, Argentina and Germany – applied to host the 1942 World Cup to be allocated at the next FIFA conference in Luxembourg in 1940 and 1942 series fell victim to the outbreak of war in 1939. Internationalism and everything FIFA represented were shattered.

FIFA's Secretary at this time, Dr Ivo Schricker, a German, managed to keep the office going in Zurich during the hostilities, and continental members of the executive managed to meet several times. Spain, Switzerland, Portugal and Sweden played each other in the war, and even the Germans managed a limited international programme until 1942. The prized FIFA trophy was put into the safe of the Italian FA, but when the Germans finally occupied Rome in 1943 after the Italian surrender, General Vaccaro, the equivalent of the Italian Sports Minister and organiser of the 1934 Tournament, and Giovanni Mauro, a former lawyer and later a referee, had the piece of gold secretly sent to a Swiss bank.

It was to take long years of work and hardship to carve a new Europe out of the ashes left by war. For FIFA, too, it was a time of renewal and reappraisal. In 1946 the FIFA congress met in Luxembourg, and the British associations were now present. Two resolutions were passed: the tournament should be given to Brazil, as South America had largely been unaffected by the ravages of war, and the World Cup statuette should be officially named the 'Jules Rimet Trophy'.

1950: Pools, Shocks, Excitement and a Samba

Brazil and its people were by now disciples of the game and fanatical in getting the show on the road. They built the huge and famous Maracana stadium in Rio on the banks of the Little Maracana River, a ground capable of holding 200,000 spectators. The final was to be watched by 199,000 people, to this day a world record football crowd.

Thirty-three teams entered what was in many ways an extraordinary competition with exciting dynamic

football. There were the usual withdrawals: Argentina quarrelled with Brazil. Austria, Belgium and Burma cancelled their entries and of the sixteen finalists, Scotland, Turkey and India pulled out. India's withdrawal was for the oddest reason – they were most upset at FIFA's insistence that their players should wear boots! France (although they had lost their qualifying place in their group to Yugoslavia) and Portugal were asked to fill the vacant spaces, but only France agreed. But because of adverse results with an experimental side before the finals, they eventually declined to grace the tournament with their presence. In any case, they disliked the idea of the travelling they would have to endure in these finals. One match would have been in Porto Alegre, followed by the next in Recife, two thousand miles away.

Henri Delaunay, Rimet's fellow pioneer, resigned before this World Cup, for he could not suffer the new idea of playing the tournament in four pools rather than on a knock-out basis as before. The four winners

Facing page: Uruguay's Maspoli watches a Brazilian shot go wide in the 1950 World Cup final.
Above: England's first World Cup team, Brazil 1950.

from each of the pools would then each play the other in the final pool matches. Points would decide the winners: two for a win, and one for a draw.

One of the biggest surprises of the tournament was England's quick exit. After winning the first match in her group against Chile 2-0, she lost to Spain 1-0 and in between to the USA 1-0. This last result was a tremendous shock, against a rag-tag assortment of players captained by Eddie McIlvenny, a Scotsman.

Another shock was the success of the new Swedish team managed by a little Yorkshireman, George Raynor. With astonishing speed he had put together a squad that not only qualified, but came third in this tournament. He was much loved and admired by his players although he had been a very moderate player himself, turning out for lowly British Football League teams such as Aldershot and Rotherham. But Stanley Rous, the then secretary of the English FA, encouraged Raynor to go to Sweden, after noticing his success in Baghdad, where he had organised an international team with lightning speed.

Brazil, as hosts, were not surprisingly a determined side, and boasted gifted players along with a coach, Costa, who was determined to lift gold. It was no small help to them that they were to play five out of their six matches in the Maracana Stadium. Goals were plentiful in these finals. The highest number scored was Uruguay's eight against Bolivia. Brazil scored 22 in six matches, including seven against Sweden and six against Spain. The deciding match in the pools was Brazil versus Uruguay. Today it is remembered as *the* World Cup match, although this tournament had not provided for it. It just happened to be the final game which would, by chance, decide the outright winner in the final pool matches. But what a magnificent game it was, a glorious climax, a thrilling showpiece. Brazil were 10-1 favourites, and already a celebratory samba had been written and recorded called 'Brazil the Victors'. The huge crowd crammed the stadium and were shocked into silence, mass faintings, mass hysterics, even suicide. The samba was left unplayed. Uruguay beat the sparkling Brazilian side 2-1.

£600,000 was taken. FIFA smiled. Nobody could deny this sort of reaction. The World Cup had bounced back to an unparalled reception.

1954: Television Captures the 'Battle of Berne'

Switzerland were the hosts for 1954, and travelling for the sixteen competing finalists was far less complicated than in the previous competition. Not so FIFA's new and complex eliminating scheme in the tournament. This time the finalists were split again into groups of four, but it was decided that two countries in each group were to be seeded and would not meet. Seedings had been worked out before the teams qualified. Spain, seeded, did not get through, so Turkey were seeded in their place above Germany. This proved to Germany's advantage. Though losing 8-3 to Hungary, they forced a play-off with Turkey who were level on points and qualified for the quarter-finals. Germany had been welcomed back to FIFA in 1950 but for this tournament were low on the list of contenders.

The Swiss tournament was not particularly efficiently organised, but television covered the event for the first time, and it was a first-class introduction for the limited viewing public. Goal-scoring was plentiful, and in 26 games there were 140 goals, an average of over five per game.

Never has a World Cup had such hotter-than-hot favourites from the kick-off. Mighty Hungary was a team of footballing stars, with the legendary Puskas as their captain. Teamwork and discipline formed the key to the Hungarians' success, for Iron Curtain countries took the finest talent available, put them into uniform and formed an army team, in this case Honved. All but one member of this World Cup team played for Honved. England and Scotland were

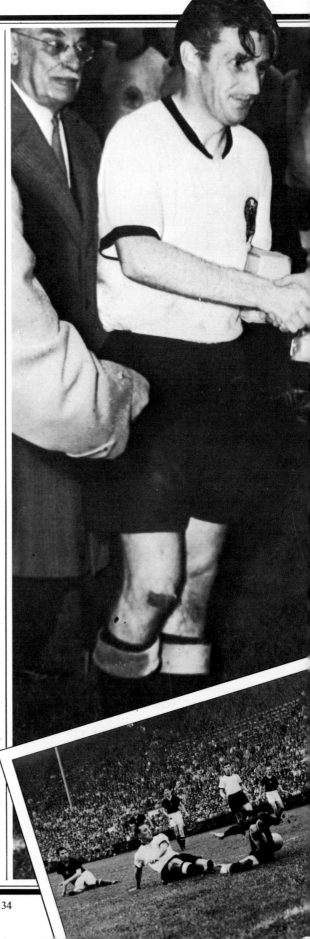

Goal scoring was plentiful in 1954: in 26 games there were 140 goals, an average of over five per game

present, England not as strong as in the past but still fielding Matthews, Finney, Lofthouse and an excellent captain in Billy Wright. Scotland was represented by a weak team and even Brazil arrived without their full complement of talent. Yugoslavia were still strong and France looked a firm set-up. Italy were a broken team: Pozzo had gone, and discipline and confidence had disappeared.

Excitement and drama throughout the finals was not lacking, however. Hungary hammered 17 goals in their first two matches, nine against Korea and eight against Germany. Turkey scored seven against little Korea and then lost to Germany 7-2 in the play-off of Pool 2. Uruguay crushed Scotland 7-0 and England reached the quarter-finals only to be accounted for by Uruguay as well, 4-2. Italy went out in the early stages, Switzerland emerging victorious 4-1 in a play-off. West German players gritted their teeth and muscled determinedly to the quarter-finals.

The final stages of this tournament formed a knock-out competition. Hungary was involved in the worst game of the tournament, then the best and ultimately the final itself. Brazil against Hungary, now known as 'The Battle of Berne', is probably the worst example of violence on and off the pitch in a World Cup game. It was a brawl and only excellent refereeing by Arthur Ellis saw it to its completion. Bozsik was dismissed from the pitch with two Brazilians. Hungary finally mastered Brazil 4-2, but the on-pitch fighting continued in the dressing rooms below with bottles. There were immediate moves to ban Brazil, who in hindsight were seen as the more guilty team, and attempts were even made to end the World Cup altogether. However, the hysteria quickly died down.

Hungary against Uruguay in the semi-final was in complete contrast to this and the match is still rated as one of the most outstanding in any World Cup. Hungary won 4-2 in torrential rain and a sea of mud. West Germany, in their semi-final, rushed to a 6-1 victory over an Austrian team which simply fell apart. The Germans showed that they could play incisive, sweeping football after all.

The Wankdorf Stadium held the final, which was

Top: Puskas (right) congratulates the winning captain Fritz Walter after West Germany had beaten Hungary in the 1954 final. Jules Rimet looks on.
Below left: Morlock nets Germany's first in the final.
Below right: Tom Finney and Nat Lofthouse take on the Uruguayan defence in a dramatic moment from 1954.

played on a rainy Sunday to a crowd of 60,000. Hungary gambled and played an unfit Puskas. His presence helped his team to make a devastating start, however, for within eight minutes they had scored twice and West Germany looked demoralised. But with their determination tempered with talent, they had swept back to 2-2 by half-time. By full-time they had won 4-2 and Hungarian pride felt as injured as Puskas physically looked.

In pouring rain Jules Rimet presented West Germany with the gold trophy. Rimet had shown the world, through the compelling eyes of television, a stunning tournament. Now he was ready to retire.

1958: Team Tactics and a New System

This tournament – now looked back on nostalgically as marking the end of a simpler, less frenetic era in football – was given to Sweden now that the Swedish Federation had admitted shamateurism and gone over to professional football played by professional footballers. Raynor was called back to take charge. He was a happy manager with a happy team and in this manner Sweden were to scale the heights of World Cup football.

Fifty-three nations entered for a place in the finals.

Facing page: Brazil on their lap of honour in 1958.
Above: Garrincha crosses for Vava (No 20) to score the equaliser for Brazil in the 1958 final.

Russia was there for the first time and so was Northern Ireland. France returned with fresh and surprising results. So too did a well-behaved and richly talented Brazilian team, who introduced to the world a young Pele surrounded by names such as Didi, Zito, Garrincha and Zagalo. They also introduced to football a new system, 4-2-4. Here was planned football, four forwards, two mid-field players, and four men in defence, a system which as played by

Brazil made for entertainment. The footballing world took note. Team tactics were of paramount importance for all the national teams and they were beginning to replace the individual's exploits on the pitch. This was the beginning of the end of an era.

1958 also marked the end of the great Hungarian team of the past and saw a sadly depleted England. Hungary, the proud and mighty finalists from 1954, had suffered the loss of their key players after the 1956 Hungarian uprising. Some were expatriates – Puskas and Kocsis had exiled themselves. The team that arrived was a parody of the once-great side. England had been badly hurt by the Munich air disaster in February 1958, when the Manchester United side was decimated. This tragic air crash killed eight key club players, internationals Byrne, Edwards and Taylor amongst them. Matthews and Finney were considered too old and were dropped. Morale, not surprisingly, was low.

France started in devastating form by beating Paraguay 7-3 and eleven goals saw them through to the quarter-finals. Their free-scoring football netted 23 goals altogether in this tournament and their star player Just Fontaine found the target thirteen times. Northern Ireland and Wales reached the knock-out stage of the tournament but England failed 1-0 in a play-off with Russia, Hungary were out but didn't shame themselves; they won their penultimate match against Mexico 4-0, but lost the play-off against Wales 2-1. Brazil excited the world public and marched confidently to the quarter-finals, and so did little Sweden. The Swedish crowds began to get very patriotic as game after game was won. The nation was beginning to believe Raynor's promise 'We're slow, but we'll reach the final'.

The semi-finals arrived and the strong West Germans were there, Brazil danced through, goal-happy France arrived and Sweden had mastered the Russians. Now Sweden were to meet the West Germans in Gothenburg. The chants of *'Heja! Heja! Heja!'* swirled around the stadium, the crowd incited to fervent patriotism by frisking cheer-leaders. At half-time the score was 1-1 and in the second half Sweden scored twice more. The 'Tortoise Team' had won a famous race and reached the final. So did Brazil, who ran riot in a 5-2 victory.

In crowd terms, the final in Stockholm was a quiet affair. The World Cup committee strictly forbade any cheerleaders on the pitch, and the Swedish crowd cowed to the stricture and created little atmosphere for their astonishing team. But on the pitch the match was anything but docile. David was meeting Goliath, and within four minutes Brazil were one down, the first time they had been in arrears throughout the competition. The giant tottered, then hit back quickly. At half-time Brazil led 2-1, and in the second half played some wonderfully exciting football. The third goal, by Pele, was breathtaking. Catching a high ball on his thigh in a packed penalty area, he hooked it over his head, swivelled and volleyed past a helpless 'keeper. Sweden got a consolation second goal but the final result stood at 5-2 – exciting, explosive stuff.

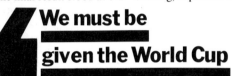

'We must be given the World Cup because we have nothing'

The Swedes were still happy, though, and the Brazilians overjoyed. For the crowd chorusing 'Samba! Samba!' the best team had won the World Cup. Brazil's golden days had arrived at last with the presentation of the Rimet Trophy by FIFA's new president, Arthur Drewry.

1962: The Cautious Sixties Arrive

A broken country was the host in 1962. Two years earlier, Chile had been torn apart by a series of major earthquakes, and Carlos Dittborn, President of the Chilean Football Federation, was aware of the commercial and political advantages of staging a World Cup competition, and pleaded his country's case with FIFA, coining the memorable phrase, 'We must be given the World Cup because we have nothing'. The FIFA Committee sympathised and by 1962 a fine stadium was built in Santiago. Another, smaller but just as good, sprang up on the coast of Vina del Mar. Splendid team quarters were supplied, and overall – against the odds – the organization was first class.

So too was the organization of the main contenders. Travelling, preparation, training and the playing were being planned and examined in detail. Teams were terrified of losing and most countries borrowed each other's systems and tactics to survive. Less goals were the result, only 89 in 32 matches. Even Brazil became more defensive and adopted a 4-3-3 system; however, they still looked the masters, and arrived sporting

Pele, now at 21 undoubtedly the best footballer in the world. Their team also featured Garrincha, the naturally gifted super-forward, Didi, Zagalo and Zito. New players were produced in the central defence and the footballing world knew it would be a very special team that could wrench the World Cup from the holders. Spain arrived with a deal of talent, but little cohesion. Puskas was playing with them now, joining up with di Stefano. England was present, managed by Walter Winterbottom for the country's fourth tournament. A new team was being built; Bobby Moore, Bobby Charlton and Jimmy Greaves looked useful talent and the squad had landed excellent quarters in the mountain retreat, Coya.

The West German warriors reached the final sixteen; full of tactics and physically strong, they would be a match for anyone. The giants of football, Russia, Uruguay and Yugoslavia were there, and so was a Hungarian team growing stronger year by year. Of Chile, very little was known. They were to use a 4-2-4 system and had lately achieved worthy results against Hungary. However, as the tournament

Manic support swept across this poor country for the meeting with Brazil in the semi-final. The feverish enthusiasm was to be slapped down by a completely one-sided match. Within thirty-two minutes it was Garrincha two, Chile nil. At half-time it was 2-1 and Chile had edged back into the game, at full-time it was 4-2. Brazil had mastered a team that had fought to stay alive until the last few minutes when Landa, the Chilean forward, followed Garrincha to the dressing rooms. Garrincha had been sent off for retaliating violently to a continual flow of hard tackles. Sadly, as he made his way out of the arena he was struck by a bottle and was badly cut about the head.

At Vina del Mar, a beautiful setting, Czechoslovakia won the other semi-final against Yugoslavia. The favourites in this match were out 3-1. A packed Czech defence preserved their goal in the first half, the forwards doing their stuff in the second.

Thus Brazil played Czechoslovakia again; in Group 3 they had already played a goalless draw. Pele was injured and would Garrincha be allowed to play? Sir Stanley Rous, President of FIFA, informed the media he would do. The Czechs went one goal ahead after quarter of an hour, but it was 1-1 at half-time. In the second half Brazil, without Pele and fielding a subdued Garrincha, won the World Cup 3-1. For the second consecutive time they paraded the Rimet Trophy.

A record 53 teams had participated in this world tournament. It was presided over by a greatly admired, firm yet gentle president in Sir Stanley Rous, but the football had not been particularly admirable and was anything but gentle. The desire to win had been overcome by the fear of losing.

1966: Destroyers and Hatchet Men

1966 saw a World Cup full of passion and controversy, watched by more people through television than ever before. It was also the first tournament to be won by the host nation, England. Managed by Alf Ramsey who had repeatedly announced 'England will win the World Cup', the competition was luckily graced by an exciting and memorable semi-final and final.

Teams from all over the world arrived with two burning ambitions – to win the World Cup and not to lose a match. It was a new age for international football, one of all-out defence. The hatchet man, the destroyer, the sweeper and the iron defender had arrived. Nations were spending fortunes to win the Rimet Trophy – 'success' was politically and financially a healthy word, and players could now become immensely rich. Failure was not to be tolerated.

The symbol of the modern game was the opening match at Wembley Stadium: England and Uruguay forced a painful 0-0 draw. Whatever is said about the tournament's quality, it did manage to sport the best final since 1954, a glorious climax. The old men of Brazil, with Pele a target for the iron men, were unable to cope with blanket defences and mediocre refereeing, and literally limped out of the competition in the early stages. They were not to achieve their hat-trick in the World Cup. The astonishing ability of the unknown North Koreans was one other major surprise: they

Above: Brazil carry the defeated Chile team's flag after they had won their semi-final round in 1962.
Top: Yachine, Russia's legendary goalkeeper, played in both the 1962 World Cup in Chile and in England in 1966.

unfolded, the Chilean streets were to ring out with *'Viva Chile!'* and the capital was to be galvanised by an impassioned crowd. Russia, Germany and Chile managed eight goals apiece in their approach to the quarter-finals. Brazil slipped easily into their fourth game and beat England 3-1 for a semi-final place. By this time it was apparent that world football had changed; physically tougher all round, the game had become much slower and very defensive.

Chile shocked the tournament and electrified the country with a 2-1 win over Russia. The Czechs were back, tough and fighting for a semi-final place, which they achieved by beating Hungary 1-0. Yugoslavia made up the winning quartet by managing a 1-0 win over West Germany. It was an excellent game, finesse triumphing over muscle and the Slav's short pass against the German's long.

It was a new age for international football, one of all-out defence. The hatchet man, the destroyer, the sweeper and the iron defender had arrived

ran like terriers and achieved much popularity amongst spectators.

Hungary arrived full of tactics and talent. Portugal on the other hand did not look so promising, but with Eusebio in their team, they had one of the game's true stars. An inside forward with a mighty scoring right foot and tremendous acceleration, he was both graceful and powerful – Europe had found a true talent to rival Pele. The team contained several other stars from the famous Benfica team: Jose Augusto, Torres and tiny Simoes. Argentina brought their ruthless defensive tactics which had already proved successful in the 1964 Brazilian International tournament. West Germany looked strong and possible winners. Seeler was to play again with an artificial Achilles tendon, and in midfield they had an abundance of young talent including a young attacking midfield player from Bayern Munich, Franz Beckenbauer. Russia were full of purpose, and though lacking in flair, they still played their goalkeeper extraordinary, Lev Yachine. After 24 matches, cruelly defensive tactics, and only 58 goals, the quarter-finals were to be played out. Now the enormously popular Koreans were to meet Portugal and the vast World Cup audience was willing them a semi-final place. At Everton, the crowd and media went wild when the Koreans snapped up three goals in the first twenty minutes without reply. Sir Stanley Rous had warned before the tournament that this Korean team was not to be taken lightly. The fairy story beginning had a realistic ending, though, with Eusebio and company winning 5-3. Hungary, after looking good, simply fell to pieces by the odd goal in three against the Russian's physical power.

The West Germany-Uruguay match was an ugly affair, two Uruguayans being sent off for kicking and

Clockwise from top right: 1966 World Cup in England: Pele signs autographs for young supporters.
Her Majesty the Queen, flanked by Prince Philip and Sir Stanley Rous, at the opening ceremony at Wembley.
The morning after: Bobby Charlton reads newspaper accounts of England's victory.
Eusebio celebrates Torres' goal against Bulgaria.
Centre: Bobby Moore holds the Rimet trophy aloft.

retaliating. Germany were not blameless but they did genuinely suffer much 'ungentlemanly behaviour.' They won 4-0 against nine men, Beckenbauer and Seeler having fine games.

The England-Argentina match was a tragedy for this World Cup and international football for years to come, creating an unhealing rift between European and South American football. If only Argentina had gone out to play football and been controlled by a good referee, they might have beaten a plodding England, who had the advantage of playing their fourth successive home match at Wembley. Rattin was sent off, and there were outrageous scenes before he finally left the pitch. England eventually managed a goal and scraped into the semi-final. After the match, the referee, Herr Kreitlein, was attacked by Argentinian reserves, players spat at linesmen and others urinated in the dressing room corridors. All this was too much for Ramsey who said, 'Our best football will come against a team which comes to play football and not act as animals' – fateful words which burn strongly in South America today.

It is an interesting fact that in this tournament all but one player sent off were playing against Germany.

When they met Russia at Everton, it was no game. Rather was it a bitter and wretched affair, once more poorly supervised by the referee. One man did stand above it: Russia's goal-keeping legend, Yachin. His brilliance kept Germany out of his goal for long periods. Russia had one player sent off, another injured when they were already one goal down and it took a mighty length of time for Germany to score again through Beckenbauer. Depleted, Russia scored in the last two minutes. On the strength of this match Germany hardly deserved to be in the final. England's fifth Wembley match was in complete contrast: a fine game against the new 'Angels of Portugal', for the 'Bashers of Brazil' came and played football. As Ramsey had promised England rose to the challenge; 2-1 was the result, and England had gained a convincing win with highly entertaining, star performances from Bobby Charlton, hatchet-man Nobby Stiles, captain Bobby Moore and the excellent Gordon Banks. Portugal had their stars too and at the end Eusebio left the hallowed turf in tears, for his side had played fine football. The game contained one extraordinary incident: when Bobby Charlton scored England's second goal, Portuguese players shook him by the

'Our best football will come against a team which comes to play football and not act as animals'

Left: Sir Alf Ramsey encourages goalkeeper Bonetti as other England players brace themselves for extra time in the 1970 quarter-final against West Germany.
Top: Mexico World Cup illuminations in Mexico City, 1970.
Above: Pele goes for goal against Italy in the final.

hand as he walked from the goal area!

The final arrived and by now, every Englishman the length and breadth of the country believed in Ramsey's words 'We will win the World Cup!' So England did and what an exciting and controversial final to the tournament it was. Helmut Schoen, the German gentleman manager, inspired his team to play football this time. England walked out on to the emerald-green pitch for the sixth time knowing that in 65 years

Germany had yet to beat them. They were confident, but this was jolted and Wembley was hushed when after thirteen minutes Haller scored for Germany. But within six minutes Hurst had headed an equaliser and this was the half-time score. The second half was breathtaking and twelve minutes from the end, Peters shot and scored. With one minute remaining and Wembley chanting 'Ee-ay-addio England's won the cup!' Germany equalised again through Weber during a goal-mouth frenzy following a German free kick outside the penalty area. Two exhausted teams collapsed on to the turf, for extra time had to be played. Ramsey, on the pitch with his players, is reported to have said 'Look at them, they're finished. You've won the World Cup once, now win it again!' Adrenalin was pumped in from somewhere and England did win by one highly controversial goal and another which by the rule book should not have been

43

allowed. Hurst scored the third which rebounded from the underside of the cross-bar and to this day cannot be proved a goal or not. The fourth, with the final kick of the match, came whilst three small boys had invaded the pitch anticipating the final whistle. Correctly, play should have been stopped with spectators on the field. However, Hurst had scored the first hat-trick in a World Cup final. The hosts had won, and the nation that had taught the world football at last held gold.

But what lessons had World Cup football learned? Would most teams continue frighteningly physical and defensive tactics, with four defenders and a sweeper behind them, three in midfield and only two forward? Was it the end of jinking, speeding wingers? Would refereeing continue to be indecisive and confused in execution? Mexico would hold the answers and in the meantime pundits and fans would have to hope. Cures must be found.

1970: Substitutes in Thin Air

Rioting, the altitude and the heat were the main worries from the moment FIFA had announced, at their congress in Tokyo, that Mexico would be the hosts for the 1970 tournament. The withering heat and breathing difficulties expected at playing heights of seven thousand feet looked dangerous. Footballers could melt in the mid-day sun and the thin air could damage their health. However, with good medical preparation the tournament went off without incident and the only worry turned out to be FIFA's new substitute rule.

Brazil would be playing in conditions admirably suited to them and were convinced they could lift the trophy for the third time – and consequently keep it for ever. Zagalo, their former player, was the new manager, Pele was still there, and so too were Gerson, Rivelino, Jairzinho and Tostao. England, the holders, were strong possibles to return victorious, if like other European teams they could overcome the conditions. They arrived in early May to prepare themselves. Moore was England's calm 'general' but he, and the entire England team, were to suffer continually from the Mexican's inhospitality and the near rioting outside their hotel before the meeting with Brazil in the Group 3 qualifying match. West Germany were in contention, Uwe Seeler would be celebrating his fourth World Cup appearance, Beckenbauer was captain, and the new Gerd Muller was a lethal centre-forward. Helmut Schoen had shaped a formidable squad. Italy arrived and the Italian newspapers stated that there was one big difference between 1966 and now – Riva. Could the idea be an Italy with ten players in defence and one up front? Peru were there in strength and managed by the old Brazilian star Didi, who had a squad with talent to spare. The solid Russians were present again and they did seem to suffer from the conditions in their first game. The hosts were to advance from Group 1 to meet Italy in the quarter-finals.

The opening games of the tournament proved that, in general, the conditions seemed to have little effect on players. Football with all its strategies was looking fresher, and refereeing was firm if fussy at times. By and large, it was a clean and sporting World Cup, but

Mexico, 1970

> ## In temperatures of over 95° even the 'mad dogs' of England should not have gone out in the midday sun

playing at noon for the sake of European television coverage was a ludicrous concession by FIFA. In temperatures of over 95° even the 'mad dogs' of England should not have gone 'out in the midday sun', never mind compete! For this tournament, FIFA had ruled that each country could name five substitutes but only use two. In the quarter-final clash between England and West Germany, the use of substitutes for England was a nightmare: Ramsey brought on Bell for Charlton and inexplicably Hunter for Peters and his team fell apart after leading 2-0. Germany substituted wisely, charged back and won 3-2 after extra time. Gordon Banks, who had made a miracle save from Pele in the Group 3 qualifying match, sadly left the arena. Mexico played Italy and like the Chileans in 1962, sensed success. The hysteria was frightening, but at full-time there was quiet and nothing to celebrate. The Italians had had their best game yet and swept the Mexicans aside. Uruguay with the last seconds of extra time ticking away managed a doubtful goal against Russia. Before the little winger Cubilla crossed for Esparrago to score, the ball for all to see – except the referee and linesmen – had crossed the goal-line. Finally in Guadalajara Brazil, still the favourites, spectacularly triumphed over Peru 4-2.

The old enemies met in the semi-final, Brazil versus Uruguay. Brazil went one down, with Felix, their unpredictable goal-keeper, letting in a shot from a seemingly impossible angle. Late in the first half, Brazil equalised and the second forty-five minutes were all theirs, even though the Uruguayans became physically brutal. Pele was superb throughout and Rivelino scored from a ball immaculately served by Pele. Brazil were victors by 3-1. In Mexico City, Italy and West Germany played exciting attacking football, not a classic game, but worthy of a World Cup semi-final. Italy were leading 1-0 and three minutes of injury time had been played when the Germans struck the equaliser. The Germans lived again as they had done in the 1966 final. Extra time brought a shower of goals and the sight of Franz Beckenbauer playing with his right arm in a sling, the result of a vicious tackle. Five goals were netted in the first twenty-one minutes of extra time and Italy emerged victorious 4-3.

The final was between two countries that had won

Facing page: Official FIFA posters for the six World Cup finals 1954-74. These are now very valuable collector's items.

SUÈDE · SWEDEN · SUECIA · SCHWEDEN 8-29.6.1958

FOOTBALL
FUTBOL
FUSSBALL

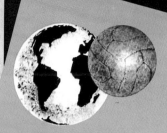

...TO MUNDIAL DE FUTBOL
...OTBALL CHAMPIONSHIP
...NAT MONDIAL DE FOOTBALL
COUPE JULES RIMET

CHILE
1962

CHAMPIONNAT DU MONDE DE FOOTBALL 1954

WORLD

MEXICO 70

IX football world championshi

may 31 – june 21

WM 74

13.6. – 7.7.1974
Hamburg   Düsseldorf   Frankfurt
West-Berlin Gelsenkirchen   Stuttgart
Hannover   Dortmund   München

FIFA World Cup 1974

WORLD CUP

JULY 11 to 30
1966
ENGLAND

'...the perfect example of 'total football': its sheer vitality, urgency and skill kept a television audience of over a billion glued to their sets'

the coveted trophy twice each. Brazil were clear favourites, but Italy had found their form and a taste for goals in the last two matches. They lost their appetite in the final. In fact, they played a negative game of all-out defence. In contrast, Brazil's flair, talent and sheer enjoyment was breathtaking to watch. Pele had a stunning farewell to offer the World Cup – he scored a brilliant first goal, exploding into the sky high above the Italian defenders and heading power-fully into the net. He went on to create two of the next three goals. Brazil won 4-1, and in so doing reminded the world that football was a game to be enjoyed even on this level. Gerson, Rivelino, Carlos Alberto, Tostao and Pele had demonstrated that South American-style football could beat the defen-sive European approach. It was the destruction of the destroyers, and European football was taught a lesson.

The Brazilians had won the Jules Rimet Trophy three times and, as FIFA had decreed, it was now theirs in perpetuity. Never did a country deserve the trophy more.

1974: Total Football

In 1972, West Germany had hosted a bloody Olympics that shocked the world and the shadow hung heavily over the lead-up to this World Cup. Security was heavier than ever but somehow there was an under-lying feeling that such a disaster could not strike twice. Ninety-nine nations had qualified and the usual sixteen arrived – fighting even before the kick-off for every penny that could be scraped from the rich money-barrels of the tournament. This World Cup was full of cash incentives for nations, teams, and players – commercialism to the nth degree had arrived. It is suspected that the West Germans had received £10,000 each by the end, the Dutch possibly twice as much. The sponsors were there and the whole finals were in the arena of big money. This time the tourna-ment was to be played throughout on a league basis, divided into four groups, the two winners in each group moving into two further groups and the winners of these two meeting in the final. Consequently there would be more matches, but no knock-out excitement

in the quarter and semi-finals. However, there was to be excitement in the stadiums, as in the intervening years since 1970, Brazil's lessons had been absorbed and – at an international level at least – a new adventurous style arrived, with Holland and Poland in particular being skilled exponents of this approach. They brought flair and skill and some adventure; this type of football was designated 'total football' – not easily translatable but basically meaning that every player on the field except the goalkeeper was a potential scorer, and all were defenders.

England had failed to reach the final sixteen, excluded following their 1-1 draw with Poland at Wembley the previous November. There was no Russia, Belgium, Switzerland, Portugal, Czecho-slovakia or Spain either. But several lesser nations elbowed their way in: little Haiti, the Third World – represented by Zaire – and even the Australians – the 'Jumping Socceroos'.

Brazil and Yugoslavia opened the proceedings with what was becoming a traditional start to a World Cup, a 0-0 draw. Played in pouring rain, Brazil looked a

Top left: England's globetrotting mascot Ken Bailey.
Top right: Opening ceremony of the 1966 World Cup.
Above: Beckenbauer scores for West Germany against England in the 1970 quarter-final match, watched by a tense crowd in Leon. Germany came back from being two down to equalise at the end of normal time and scored the winning goal in extra time.
Above left: Brazil supporters in the mood for victory at the 1970 final.

patched-up team without Pele, Carlos Alberto, Tostao and Gerson – Yugoslavia gave warning that muscle was around once more. Scotland were present and battled hard to reach the next groupings. They failed but played far better than expected, didn't lose a match and only conceded one goal. They went out on statistics. Goal-scoring was to reach its lowest ebb with only 97 goals in 38 matches, despite Yugoslavia hammering nine against Zaire – during which a player from the African team was sent off for kicking. The exciting Poles knocked seven past Haiti but the Australians did not make any real impact.

The Dutch team led by Cruyff at first seemed to be in a shambles, but they soon pulled themselves together and were to play wonderful 'total football'. They danced around the bludgeoning Uruguayans in one match, winning 2-0 when it could have been 12-0. West Germany galloped on with holes in their defence but attacking football in mind. Sweden brought back golden memories by a surprising win against Uruguay and holding Holland to a 0-0 draw. They were now serious contenders.

The second round arrived – poor, dull and destructive teams had been eliminated. Holland, Brazil and East Germany – who on the way had been victorious over fellow qualifiers West Germany 1-0 – survived. The exciting-looking Poles and gutsy Swedes were there and Argentina and Yugoslavia had battled through. The matches were livening up and the most successful teams in the tournament were employing a delicate balance of attack and defence, moving swiftly out of defence at the first opportunity but with caution, for modern football's priorities still leaned to defence.

The Dutch now came into their own and so did their players: Cruyff, the star of the tournament, Rep, Neeskens, Krol. They tore into Argentina 4-0, and the destroyers were destroyed again, though in fairness the Argentinians, with hosting the 1978 finals in mind, left behind a better-than-usual impression of themselves. West Germany now believed in their football and showed it against Yugoslavia and Sweden. They scored four goals against Sweden who got a couple in return. Brazil were to go; they had suffered from underestimating the European upsurge in attacking play as well as losing their aged stars. The Poles took third place in the tournament, when expected to achieve nothing. The trophy slipped out of their grasp in pouring rain against the West Germans, and one goal scored by Muller decided the match.

The new league system for 1974 produced an ideal Cup Final: West Germany versus Holland, the two most overtly entertaining teams in the world. Before the kick-off the Dutch were looked on as the favourites and by the opening minute of the game had converted a penalty and were fulfilling all expectations. This ninety minutes was the perfect example of 'total football': its sheer vitality, urgency and skill kept a television audience of over a billion glued to their sets. The final result was 2-1 to the Germans, who had equalled the Dutch flair in every way, raising their game and attaining heights of skill that surprised even the most ardent of German supporters. Beckenbauer was an inspiration and Muller, though a marked man, was outstanding and managed to score the winning goal after Breitner had equalised with the second penalty of the match.

In organisation and style the World Cup had come of age. In a very real way now, the dreams of Rimet and the founders of FIFA were truly fulfilled – their 1974 tournament had been played in a spirit of goodwill and sportsmanship. This was endorsed by the very moving closing ceremony in the Munich stadium when hundreds of children, each holding a rose, broke into song.

1978: The Eleventh World Cup

It must be hoped that in Argentina, the significance of those roses is upheld by the generals and their military *junta*. There is every reason to believe that it will be, for the country is determined to present a fresh

> **Four years has usually been the maximum that any country could sustain a level of performance capable of winning such a major honour**

face to the world and hold a memorable and sporting tournament.

What of the competing nations? There will be one or two surprises present, but in general, the usual global power-houses of football will be competing.

Although it can be said that the best overall standard of good footballers must still lie in England, it will be a surprise to find this proud footballing nation in the final sixteen. It is a sad fact that the world continues to want and indeed expects England's presence, and yet there could now be a gap of twelve years before the 'teachers' once more compete.

The most talented individual players are certainly to be found elsewhere: in South America, particularly in Brazil, a nation that should once again be exciting and at times magical to watch. The eastern bloc will be interesting to observe, as more and more they are vying with the West Germans and the Dutch. Here are two nations who are probably still the biggest threat if they can continue their recent standards. Both have continued to produce the quality all-purpose players needed for the 'every player can attack and every player can defend' principle. This is brave football and will continue to be played by Holland and West Germany. It is to be hoped shades of it will be seen in other nations' play – Poland showed signs of this exciting approach in Munich. In complete contrast, Italy seem unlikely to change: their concept of play is strictly defensive, with the minimum of attacking play.

Will all the favourites fall this time? Could the unexpected really happen? On the one hand, on all previous occasions when the World Cup has been held in the Americas it has been won by South American countries. On the other, four years has usually been the maximum that any country could manage to sustain a level of performance capable of winning such a major honour and undoubtedly it would be a tremendous effort to succeed again.

Could a David slay Goliath? In the drama and excitement of football's biggest showcase and with talent and skill catching like wildfire right across the footballing nations, much is possible in the Game of the Century.

URUGUAY 1930

POOL 1

France 4, Mexico 1 (T 3/0)
Argentina 1, France 0 (HT 0/0)
Chile 3, Mexico 0 (HT 1/0)
Chile 1, France 0 (HT 0/0)
Argentina 6, Mexico 3 (HT 3/0)
Argentina 3, Chile 1 (HT 2/1)

					GOALS		
	P	W	D	L	F	A	Pts
Argentina	3	3	0	0	10	4	6
Chile	3	2	0	1	5	3	4
France	3	1	0	2	4	3	2
Mexico	3	0	0	3	4	13	0

POOL 2

Yugoslavia 2, Brazil 1 (HT 2/0)
Yugoslavia 4, Bolivia 0 (HT 0/0)
Brazil 4, Bolivia 0 (HT 1/0)

					GOALS		
	P	W	D	L	F	A	Pts
Yugoslavia	2	2	0	0	6	1	4
Brazil	2	1	0	1	5	2	2
Bolivia	2	0	0	2	0	8	0

POOL 3

Romania 3, Peru 1 (HT 1/0)
Uruguay 1, Peru 0 (HT 0/0)
Uruguay 4, Romania 0 (HT 4/0)

					GOALS		
	P	W	D	L	F	A	Pts
Uruguay	2	2	0	0	5	0	4
Romania	2	1	0	1	3	5	2
Peru	2	0	0	2	1	4	0

POOL 4

United States 3, Belgium 0 (HT 2/0)
United States 3, Paraguay 0 (HT 2/0)
Paraguay 1, Belgium 0 (HT 1/0)

					GOALS		
	P	W	D	L	F	A	Pts
United States	2	2	0	0	6	0	4
Paraguay	2	1	0	1	1	3	3
Belgium	2	0	0	2	0	4	0

SEMI-FINALS

ARGENTINA 6
Botasso; Della Torre;
Paternoster; Evaristo, J.;
Monti; Orlandini;
Peucelle; Scopelli; Stabile;
Ferreira (capt.);
Evaristo, M.

UNITED STATES 1
Douglas; Wood;
Moorhouse; Gallacher;
Tracey; Auld; Brown;
Gonsalvez; Patenaude;
Florie (capt,); McGhee.

SCORERS

Monti, Scopelli, Stabile (2), Peucelle (2), for Argentina
Brown for United States
HT 1/0

URUGUAY 6
Ballesteros; Nasazzi (capt.);
Mascheroni; Andrade;
Fernandez; Gestido;
Dorado; Scarone;
Anselmo; Cea; Iriarte.

YUGOSLAVIA 1
Yavocic; Ivkovic (capt.);
Milhailovic; Arsenievic;
Stefanovic; Djokic;
Tirnanic; Marianovic;
Beck; Vujadinovic; Seculic.

SCORERS

Cea (3), Anselmo (2), Iriarte for Uruguay
Seculic for Yugoslavia
HT 3/1

FINAL

URUGUAY 4
Ballesteros; Nasazzi (capt.);
Mascheroni; Andrade;
Fernandez; Gestido;
Dorado; Scarone;
Castro; Cea; Iriarte.

ARGENTINA 2
Botasso; Della Torre;
Paternoster; Evaristo, J;
Monti; Suarez; Peucelle;
Varallo; Stabile; Ferreira;
(capt.); Evaristo, M.

SCORERS

Dorado, Cea, Iriarte, Castro for Uruguay
Peucelle, Stabile for Argentina
HT 1/2

ITALY 1934

FIRST ROUND

Italy 7, United States 1 (HT 3/0)
Czechoslovakia 2, Romania 1 (HT 0/1)
Germany 5, Belgium 2 (HT 1/2)
Austria 3, France 2 (HT 1/1, 1/1) after extra time
Spain 3, Brazil 1 (HT 3/1)
Switzerland 3, Holland 2 (HT 2/1)
Sweden 3, Argentina 2 (HT 1/1)
Hungary 4, Egypt 2 (HT 2/1)

SECOND ROUND

Germany 2, Sweden 1 (HT 1/0)
Austria 2, Hungary 1 (HT 1/0)
Italy 1, Spain 1 (HT 1/0, 1/1) after extra time
Italy 1, Spain 0 (HT 1/0) Replay
Czechoslovakia 3, Switzerland 2 (HT 1/1)

SEMI-FINALS

ROME

CZECHOSLOVAKIA 3
Planicka (capt.); Burger;
Ctyroky; Kostalek;
Cambal, Krcil; Junek;
Svoboda; Sobotka;
Nejedly; Puc.

GERMANY 1
Kress; Haringer; Busch;
Zielinski; Szepan (capt.);
Bender; Lehner; Siffling;
Conen; Noack;
Kobierski.

SCORERS

Nejedly (2), Krcil for Czechoslovakia
Noack for Germany
HT 1/0

MILAN

ITALY 1
Combi (capt.);
Monzeglio; Allemandi;
Ferraris IV; Monti;
Bertolini; Guaita; Meazza;
Schiavio; Ferrari; Orsi.

AUSTRIA 0
Platzer; Cisar; Seszta;
Wagner; Smistik (capt.);
Urbanek; Zischek; Bican;
Sindelar; Schall; Viertel.

SCORER

Guaita for Italy
HT 1/0

THIRD PLACE MATCH
NAPLES

GERMANY 3
Jakob; Janes; Busch; Zielinski; Muenzenberg; Bender; Lehner; Siffling; Conen; Szepan (capt.); Heidemann.

AUSTRIA 2
Platzer; Cisar; Seszta; Wagner; Smistik (capt.); Urbanek; Zischek; Braun; Bican; Horwath; Viertel.

SCORERS

Lehner (2), Conen for Germany
Seszta for Austria
HT 3/1

FINAL
ROME

ITALY 2
(after extra time)
Combi (capt.); Monzeglio; Allemandi; Ferraris IV; Monti; Bertolini; Guaita; Meazza; Schiavio; Ferrari; Orsi.

CZECHOSLOVAKIA 1
Planicka (capt.); Zenisek; Ctyroky; Kostalek; Cambal; Krcil; Junek; Svoboda; Sobotka; Nejedly; Puc.

SCORERS

Orsi, Schiavio for Italy
Puc for Czechoslovakia
HT 0/0

FRANCE 1938

FIRST ROUND

Switzerland 1, Germany 1 (HT 1/1, 1/1) after extra time
Switzerland 4, Germany 2 (HT 0/2) replay
Cuba 3, Romania 3 (HT 0/1, 3/3) after extra time
Cuba 2, Romania 1 (HT 0/1) replay
Hungary 6, Dutch East Indies 0 (HT 4/0)
France 3, Belgium 1 (HT 2/1)
Czechoslovakia 3, Holland 0 (HT 0/0, 0/0) after extra time

Brazil 6, Poland 5 (HT 3/1, 4/4) after extra time
Italy 2, Norway 1 (HT 1/0, 1/1) after extra time

SECOND ROUND

Sweden 8, Cuba 0 (HT 4/0)
Hungary 2, Switzerland 0 (HT 1/0)
Italy 3, France 1 (HT 1/1)
Brazil 1, Czechoslovakia 1 (HT 1/1, 1/1) after extra time
Brazil 2, Czechoslovakia 1 (HT 0/1) replay

SEMI-FINALS
MARSEILLES

ITALY 2
Olivieri; Foni; Rava; Serantoni; Andreolo; Locatelli; Biavati; Meazza (capt.); Piola; Ferrari; Colaussi.

BRAZIL 1
Walter; Domingas; Da Guia; Machados; Zeze; Martin (capt.); Alfonsinho; Lopez; Luisinho; Peracio; Romeo; Patesko.

SCORERS

Colaussi, Meazza (penalty) for Italy
Romeo for Brazil
HT 2/0

PARIS

HUNGARY 5
Szabo; Koranyi; Biro; Szalay; Turai; Lazar; Sas; Szengeller; Sarosi (capt.); Toldi; Titkos.

SWEDEN 1
Abrahamson; Eriksson; Kjellgren; Almgren; Jacobsson; Svanstroem; Wetterstroem; Keller (capt.); Andersson, H.; Jonasson; Nyberg.

SCORERS

Szengeller (3), Titkos, Sarosi for Hungary
Nyberg for Sweden
HT 3/1

THIRD PLACE MATCH
BORDEAUX

BRAZIL 4
Batatoes; Domingas Da Guia; Machados; Zeze; Brandao; Alfonsinho; Roberto; Romeo; Leonidas (capt.); Peracio; Patesko.

SWEDEN 2
Abrahamson; Eriksson; Nilsson; Almgren; Linderholm; Svanstroem (capt.); Berssen; Andersson, H.; Jonasson; Andersson, A.; Nyberg.

SCORERS

Romeo, Leonidas (2), Peracio for Brazil
Jonasson, Nyberg for Sweden
HT 1/2

FINAL
PARIS

ITALY 4
Olivieri; Foni; Rava; Serantoni; Andreolo; Locatelli; Biavati; Meazza (capt.); Piola; Ferrari; Colaussi.

HUNGARY 2
Szabo; Polgar; Biro; Szalay; Szucs; Lazar; Sas; Vincze; Sarosi (capt.); Szengeller; Titkos.

SCORERS

Colaussi (2), Piola (2) for Italy
Titkos, Sarosi for Hungary
HT 3/1

BRAZIL 1950

POOLS 1, 2, 3, 4

Brazil 4, Mexico 0 (HT 1/0)
Yugoslavia 3, Switzerland 0 (HT 3/0)
Yugoslavia 4, Mexico 1 (HT 2/0)
Brazil 2, Switzerland 2 (HT 2/1)
Brazil 2, Yugoslavia 0 (HT 1/0)
Switzerland 2, Mexico 1 (HT 2/0)

	P	W	D	L	GOALS F	A	Pts
Brazil	3	2	1	0	8	2	5
Yugoslavia	3	2	0	1	7	3	4
Switzerland	3	1	1	1	4	6	3
Mexico	3	0	0	3	2	10	0

Spain 3, United States 1 (HT 0/1)
England 2, Chile 0 (HT 1/0)
United States 1, England 0 (HT 1/0)
Spain 2, Chile 0 (HT 2/0)
Spain 1, England 0 (HT 0/0)
Chile 5, United States 2 (HT 2/0)

	P	W	D	L	GOALS F	A	Pts
Spain	3	3	0	0	6	1	6
England	3	1	0	2	2	2	2
Chile	3	1	0	2	5	6	2
United States	3	1	0	2	4	8	2

Sweden 3, Italy 2 (HT 2/1)
Sweden 2, Paraguay 2 (HT 2/1)
Italy 2, Paraguay 0 (HT 1/0)

	P	W	D	L	GOALS F	A	Pts
Sweden	2	1	1	0	5	4	3
Italy	2	1	0	1	4	3	2
Paraguay	2	0	1	1	2	4	1

Uruguay 8, Bolivia 0 (HT 4/0)

	P	W	D	L	GOALS F	A	Pts
Uruguay	1	1	0	0	8	0	2
Bolivia	1	0	0	1	0	8	0

FINAL POOL MATCHES

SAO PAULO

URUGUAY 2
Maspoli; Gonzales, M.;
Tejera; Gonzales, W.;
Varela (capt.); Andrade;
Ghiggia; Perez; Miguez;
Schiaffino; Vidal.

SPAIN 2
Ramallets; Alonzo;
Gonzalvo II; Gonzalvo
III; Parra, Puchades;
Basora; Igoa; Zarra;
Molowny; Gainza.

SCORERS

Ghiggia, Varela for Uruguay
Basora (2) for Spain
HT 1/2

RIO

BRAZIL 7
Barbosa; Augusto (capt.);
Juvenal; Bauer; Danilo;
Bigode; Maneca; Zizinho;
Ademir; Jair; Chico.

SWEDEN 1
Svensson; Samuelsson;
Nilsson, E.; Andersson;
Nordahl, K.; Gard;
Sundqvist; Palmer;
Jeppson; Skoglund;
Nilsson, S.

SCORERS

Ademir (4), Chico (2), Maneca for Brazil
Andersson (penalty) for Sweden
HT 3/0

SAO PAULO

URUGUAY 3
Paz; Gonzales, M.;
Tejera; Gambetta; Varela
(capt.); Andrade; Ghiggia;
Perez; Miguez;
Schiaffino, Vidal.

SWEDEN 2
Svensson; Samuelsson;
Nilsson, E.; Andersson;
Johansson; Gard;
Johnsson; Palmer;
Melberg; Skoglund;
Sundqvist.

SCORERS

Ghiggia, Miguez (2) for Uruguay
Palmer, Sundqvist for Sweden
HT 1/2

RIO

BRAZIL 6
Barbosa; Augusto (capt.);
Juvenal; Bauer; Danilo;
Bigode; Friaca; Zizinho;
Ademir; Jair; Chico.

SPAIN 1
Eizaguirre; Alonzo;
Gonzalvo II; Gonzalvo
III; Parra; Puchades;
Basora; Igoa; Zarra;
Panizo; Gainza.

SCORERS

Jair (2), Chico (2), Zizinho, Parra (own goal) for Brazil
Igoa for Spain
HT 2/0

SAO PAULO

SWEDEN 3
Svensson; Samuelsson;
Nilsson, E.; Andersson;
Johansson; Gard;
Sundqvist; Menllberg;
Rydell; Palmer; Johnsson.

SPAIN 1
Eizaguirre; Asensi;
Alonzo; Silva; Parra;
Puchades; Basora;
Fernandez; Zarra; Panizo;
Juncosa.

SCORERS

Johansson, Mellberg, Palmer for Sweden
Zarra for Spain
HT 2/0

RIO

URUGUAY 2
Maspoli; Gonzales, M.;
Tejera; Gambetta;
Varela (capt.); Andrade;
Ghiggia; Perez; Miguez;
Schiaffino, Moran.

BRAZIL 1
Barbosa; Augusto (capt.);
Juvenal; Bauer; Danilo;
Bigode; Friaca; Zizinho;
Ademir; Jair; Chico.

SCORERS

Schiaffino, Ghiggia for Uruguay
Friaca for Brazil
HT 0/0

FINAL POSITIONS

					GOALS		
	P	W	D	L	F	A	Pts
Uruguay	3	2	1	0	7	5	5
Brazil	3	2	0	1	14	4	4
Sweden	3	1	0	2	6	11	2
Spain	3	0	1	2	4	11	1

SWITZERLAND 1954

POOL 1

Yugoslavia 1, France 0 (HT 1/0)
Brazil 5, Mexico 0 (HT 4/0)
France 3, Mexico 2 (HT 1/0)
Brazil 1, Yugoslavia 1 (HT 0/1) after extra time

					GOALS		
	P	W	D	L	F	A	Pts
Brazil	2	1	1	0	6	1	3
Yugoslavia	2	1	1	0	2	1	3
France	2	1	0	1	3	3	2
Mexico	2	0	0	2	2	8	0

POOL 2

Hungary 9, Korea 0 (HT 4/0)
Germany 4, Turkey 1 (HT 1/1)
Hungary 8, Germany 3 (HT 3/1)
Turkey 7, Korea 0 (HT 4/0)

					GOALS		
	P	W	D	L	F	A	Pts
Hungary	2	2	0	0	17	3	4
Germany	2	1	0	1	7	9	2
Turkey	2	1	0	1	8	4	2
Korea	2	0	0	2	0	16	0

Play off Germany 7, Turkey 2 (HT 3/1)

POOL 3

Austria 1, Scotland 0 (HT 1/0)
Uruguay 2, Czechoslovakia 0 (HT 0/0)
Austria 5, Czechoslovakia 0 (HT 4/0)
Uruguay 7, Scotland 0 (HT 2/0)

					GOALS		
	P	W	D	L	F	A	Pts
Uruguay	2	2	0	0	9	0	4
Austria	2	2	0	0	6	0	4
Czechoslovakia	2	0	0	2	0	7	0
Scotland	2	0	0	2	0	8	0

POOL 4

England 4, Belgium 4 (HT 2/1)
England 2, Switzerland 0 (HT 1/0)
Switzerland 2, Italy 1 (HT 1/1)
Italy 4, Belgium 1 (HT 1/0)

					GOALS		
	P	W	D	L	F	A	Pts
England	2	1	1	0	6	4	3
Italy	2	1	0	1	5	3	2
Switzerland	2	1	0	1	2	3	2
Belgium	2	0	1	1	5	8	1

Play off Switzerland 4, Italy 1 (HT 1/0)

QUARTER-FINALS

GENEVA

GERMANY 2
Turek; Laband;
Kohlmeyer; Eckel;
Liebrich; Mai; Rahn;
Morlock; Walter, O.;
Walter, F. (capt.); Schaefer.

YUGOSLAVIA 0
Beara; Stankovic;
Crnkovic; Cjaicowski, I.;
Horvat; Boskov;
Milutinovic, Mitic (capt.);
Vukas; Bobek; Zebec.

SCORERS

Horvat (own goal), Rahn for Germany
HT 1/0

BERNE

HUNGARY 4
Grosics; Buzansky;
Lantos; Bozsik (capt.);
Lorant; Zakarias; Toth, M.;
Kocsis; Hidegkuti;

BRAZIL 2
Castilho; Santos, D.;
Santos, N.; Brandaozinho;
Pinheiro (capt.); Bauer;
Julinho; Didi; Indio;

Czibor; Toth, J.   Tozzi; Maurinho.

SCORERS

Hidegkuti (2), Kocsis, Lantos (penalty) for Hungary
Santos, D. (penalty), Julinho for Brazil
HT 2/1

LAUSANNE

AUSTRIA 7
Schmied; Hanappi;
Barschandt; Ocwirk
(capt.); Happel; Koller;
Koerner, R.; Wagner;
Stojaspal; Probst;
Koerner, A.

SWITZERLAND 5
Parlier; Neury; Kernen;
Eggimann; Bocquet
(capt.); Casali; Antenen;
Vonlanthen; Hugi;
Ballaman; Fatton.

SCORERS

Koerner, A. (2), Ocwirk, Wagner (3), Probst for Austria
Ballaman (2), Hugi (2), Hanappi (own goal) for
Switzerland
HT 2/4

BASEL

URUGUAY 4
Maspoli; Santamaria;
Martinez; Andrade;
Varela (capt.); Cruz;
Abbadie; Ambrois;
Miguez; Schiaffino;
Borges.

ENGLAND 2
Merrick; Staniforth;
Byrne; McGarry; Wright
(capt.); Dickinson;
Matthews; Broadis;
Lofthouse; Wilshaw;
Finney.

SCORERS

Borges, Varela, Schiaffino, Ambrois for Uruguay
Lofthouse, Finney for England
HT 2/1

SEMI-FINALS
BASEL

GERMANY 6
Turek; Posipal;
Kohlmeyer; Eckel;
Liebrich; Mai; Rahn;
Morlock; Walter, O.;
Walter, F. (capt.);
Schaefer.

AUSTRIA 1
Zeman; Hanappi;
Schleger; Ocwirk (capt.);
Happel; Koller; Koerner;
R.; Wagner; Stojaspal;
Probst; Koerner, A.

SCORERS

Schaefer, Morlock, Walter, F. (2 penalties), Walter, O. (2)
for Germany
Probst for Austria
HT 1/0

LAUSANNE

HUNGARY 4
(after extra time)
Grosics; Buzansky;
Lantos; Boszik (capt.);
Lorant; Zakarias; Budai;
Kocsis; Palotas;
Hidegkuti; Czibor.

URUGUAY 2
Maspoli; Santamaria;
Martinez; Andrade (capt.);
Carballo; Cruz; Souto;
Ambrois; Schiaffino;
Hohberg; Borges.

SCORERS

Czibor, Hidegkuti, Kocsis (2) for Hungary
Hohberg (2) for Uruguay
HT 1/0

THIRD PLACE MATCH
ZURICH

AUSTRIA 3
Schmied; Hanappi;
Barschandt; Ocwirk
(capt.); Kollmann;
Koller; Koerner, R.;
Wagner; Dienst;
Stojaspal; Probst.

URUGUAY 1
Maspoli; Santamaria;
Martinez; Andrade;
(capt.); Carballo; Cruz;
Abbadie; Hohberg;
Mendez; Schiaffino;
Borges.

SCORERS

Stojaspal (penalty), Cruz (own goal), Ocwirk for Austria
Hohberg for Hungary
HT 1/1

FINAL
BERNE

GERMANY 3
Turek; Posipal;
Kohlmeyer; Eckel;
Liebrich; Mai; Rahn;
Morlock; Walter, O.;
Walter, F.; Schaefer.

HUNGARY 2
Grosics; Buzansky;
Lantos; Bozsik; Lorant;
Zakarias; Czibor; Kocsis;
Hidegkuti; Puskas; Toth, J.

SCORERS

Morlock, Rahn (2) for Germany
Puskas, Czibor for Hungary
HT 2/2

	P	W	D	L	GOALS F	A	Pts
France	3	2	0	1	11	7	4
Yugoslavia	3	1	2	0	7	6	4
Paraguay	3	1	1	1	9	12	3
Scotland	3	0	1	2	4	6	1

POOL 3

Sweden 3, Mexico 0 (HT 1/0)
Hungary 1, Wales 1 (HT 1/1)
Wales 1, Mexico 1 (HT 1/1)
Sweden 2, Hungary 1 (HT 1/0)
Sweden 0, Wales 0 (HT 0/0)
Hungary 4, Mexico 0 (HT 1/0)

	P	W	D	L	GOALS F	A	Pts
Sweden	3	2	1	0	5	1	5
Hungary	3	1	1	1	6	3	3
Wales	3	0	3	0	2	2	3
Mexico	3	0	1	2	1	8	1

Play off Wales 2, Hungary 1 (HT 0/1)

POOL 4

England 2, Russia 2 (HT 0/1)
Brazil 3, Austria 0 (HT 1/0)
England 0, Brazil 0 (HT 0/0)
Russia 2, Austria 0 (HT 1/0)
Brazil 2, Russia 0 (HT 1/0)
England 2, Austria 2 (HT 0/1)

	P	W	D	L	GOALS F	A	Pts
Brazil	3	2	1	0	5	0	5
England	3	0	3	0	4	4	3
Russia	3	1	1	1	4	4	3
Austria	3	0	1	2	2	7	1

Play off Russia 1, England 0 (HT 0/0)

QUARTER-FINALS
NORRKOPING

FRANCE 4
Abbes; Kaelbel; Lerond;
Penverne; Jonquet;
Marcel; Wisnieski;
Fontaine; Kopa; Piantoni;
Vincent.

IRELAND 0
Gregg; Keith; McMichael;
Blanchflower;
Cunningham; Cush;
Bingham; Casey; Scott;
McIlroy; McParland.

SCORERS

Wisnieski, Fontaine (2), Piantoni for France
HT 1/0

MALMO

WEST GERMANY 1
Herkenrath; Stollenwerk;
Juskowiak; Eckel;
Erhardt; Szymaniak;
Rahn; Walter; Seeler;
Schmidt; Schaefer.

YUGOSLAVIA 0
Krivocuka; Sijakovic;
Crnkovic; Kristic; Zebec;
Boskov; Petakovic;
Veselinovic; Milutinovic;
Ognjanovic; Rajkov.

SWEDEN 1958

POOL 1

Germany 3, Argentina 1 (HT 2/1)
Ireland 1, Czechoslovakia 0 (HT 1/0)
Germany 2, Czechoslovakia 2 (HT 1/0)
Argentina 3, Ireland 1 (HT 1/1)
Germany 2, Ireland 2 (HT 1/1)
Czechoslovakia 6, Argentina 1 (HT 3/1)

	P	W	D	L	GOALS F	A	Pts
Germany	3	1	2	0	7	5	4
Czechoslovakia	3	1	1	1	8	4	3
Ireland	3	1	1	1	4	5	3
Argentina	3	1	0	2	5	10	2

POOL 2

France 7, Paraguay 3 (HT 2/2)
Yugoslavia 1, Scotland 1 (HT 1/0)
Yugoslavia 3, France 2 (HT 1/1)
Paraguay 3, Scotland 2 (HT 2/1)
France 2, Scotland 1 (HT 2/0)
Yugoslavia 3, Paraguay 3 (HT 2/1)

Rahn for West Germany
HT 1/0

STOCKHOLM

SWEDEN 2	RUSSIA 0
Svensson; Bergmark;	Yachine; Kessarev;
Axbom; Boerjesson;	Kuznetsov, Voinov;
Gustavsson; Parling;	Krijevski; Tsarev; Ivanov,
Hamrin; Gren;	A. Ivanov, V.; Simonian;
Simonsson; Liedholm;	Salnikowllyin.
Skoglund.	

SCORERS

Hamrin, Simonsson for Sweden
HT 0/0

GOTHENBURG

BRAZIL 1	WALES 0
Gilmar; De Sordi; Santos,	Kelsey; Williams;
N.; Zito; Bellini;	Hopkins; Sullivan;
Orlando; Garrincha; Didi;	Charles, M.; Bowen;
Mazzola; Pelé; Zagalo.	Medwin; Hewitt;
	Webster; Allchurch; Jones.

SCORER

Pelé for Brazil
HT 0/0

SEMI-FINALS
STOCKHOLM

BRAZIL 5	FRANCE 2
Gilmar; De Sordi; Santos,	Abbes; Kaelbel; Lerond;
N.; Zito; Bellini;	Penverne; Jonquet;
Orlando; Garrincha; Didi;	Marcel; Wisnieski;
Vava; Pelé; Zagalo.	Fontaine; Kopa; Piantoni;
	Vincent.

SCORERS

Vava, Didi, Pelé (3) for Brazil
Fontaine, Piantoni for France
HT 2/1

GOTHENBURG

SWEDEN 3	WEST GERMANY 1
Svensson; Bergmark;	Herkenrath; Stollenwerk;
Axbom; Boerjesson;	Juskowiak; Eckel;
Gustavsson; Parling;	Erhardt; Szymaniak;
Hamrin; Gren;	Rahn; Walter; Seeler;
Simonsson; Liedholm;	Schaefer; Cieslarczyk.
Skoglund.	

SCORERS

Skoglund, Gren, Hamrin for Sweden
Schaefer for Germany
HT 1/1

THIRD PLACE MATCH
GOTHENBURG

FRANCE 6	WEST GERMANY 3
Abbes; Kaelbel; Lerond;	Kwiatowski; Stollenwerk;
Penverne; Lafont; Marcel;	Erhardt; Schnellinger;
Wisnieski; Douis; Kopa;	Wewers; Szymaniak;
Fontaine; Vincent.	Rahn; Sturm; Reipassa;
	Schaefer, Cieslarczyk.

SCORERS

Fontaine (4), Kopa (penalty), Douis for France
Cieslarezyk, Rahn, Schaefer for Germany
HT 3/1

FINAL
STOCKHOLM

BRAZIL 5	SWEDEN 2
Gilmar; Santos, D.; Santos,	Svensson; Bergmark;
N.; Zito; Bellini;	Axbom; Boerjesson;
Orlando; Garrincha; Didi;	Gustavsson; Parling;
Vava; Pelé; Zagalo.	Hamrin; Gren;
	Simonsson; Liedholm;
	Skoglund.

SCORERS

Vava (2), Pelé (2), Zagalo for Brazil
Liedholm, Simonsson for Sweden
HT 2/1

CHILE 1962
GROUP 1

Uruguay 2, Colombia 1 (HT 0/1)
Russia 2, Yugoslavia 0 (HT 0/0)
Yugoslavia 3, Uruguay 1 (HT 2/1)
Russia 4, Colombia 4 (HT 3/1)
Russia 2, Uruguay 1 (HT 1/0)
Yugoslavia 5, Colombia 0 (HT 2/0)

				GOALS		
	P	W	D	L	F	A	Pts
Russia	3	2	1	0	8	5	5
Yugoslavia	3	2	0	1	8	3	4
Uruguay	3	1	0	2	4	6	2
Colombia	3	0	1	2	5	11	1

GROUP 2

Chile 3, Switzerland 1 (HT 1/1)
Germany 0, Italy 0 (HT 0/0)
Chile 2, Italy 0 (HT 0/0)
Germany 2, Switzerland 1 (HT 1/0)
Germany 2, Chile 0 (HT 1/0)
Italy 3, Switzerland 0 (HT 1/0)

	GOALS						
	P	W	D	L	F	A	Pts
Germany	3	2	1	0	4	1	5
Chile	3	2	0	1	5	3	4
Italy	3	1	1	1	3	2	3
Switzerland	3	0	0	3	2	8	0

GROUP 3

Brazil 2, Mexico 0 (HT 0/0)
Czechoslovakia 1, Spain 0 (HT 0/0)
Brazil 0, Czechoslovakia 0 (HT 0/0)
Spain 1, Mexico 0 (HT 0/0)
Brazil 2, Spain 1 (HT 0/1)
Mexico 3, Czechoslovakia 1 (HT 2/1)

	GOALS						
	P	W	D	L	F	A	Pts
Brazil	3	2	1	0	4	1	5
Czechoslovakia	3	1	1	1	2	3	3
Mexico	3	1	0	2	3	4	2
Spain	3	1	0	2	2	3	2

GROUP 4

Argentina 1, Bulgaria 0 (HT 1/0)
Hungary 2, England 1 (HT 1/0)
England 3, Argentina 1 (HT 2/0)
Hungary 6, Bulgaria 1 (HT 4/0)
Argentina 0, Hungary 0 (HT 0/0)
England 0, Bulgaria 0 (HT 0/0)

	GOALS						
	P	W	D	L	F	A	Pts
Hungary	3	2	1	0	8	2	5
England	3	1	1	1	4	3	3
Argentina	3	1	1	1	2	3	3
Bulgaria	3	0	1	2	1	7	1

QUARTER-FINALS
SANTIAGO

YUGOSLAVIA 1
Soskic; Durkovic; Jusufi; Radakovic; Markovic; Popovic; Kovacevic; Sekularac; Jerkovic; Galic; Skoblar.

WEST GERMANY 0
Fahrian; Novak; Schnellinger; Schulz; Erhardt; Giesemann; Haller; Syzmaniak; Seeler; Brulls; Schaefer.

SCORER

Radakovic for Yugoslavia
HT 0/0

VINA DEL MAR

BRAZIL 3
Gilmar; Santos, D.; Mauro; Zozimo; Santos, N.; Zito; Didi; Garrincha; Vavà; Amarildo; Zagalo.

ENGLAND 1
Springett; Armfield; Wilson; Moore; Norman; Flowers; Douglas; Greaves; Hitchens; Haynes; Charlton.

SCORERS

Garrincha (2), Vavà for Brazil
Hitchens for England
HT 1/1

ARICO

CHILE 2
Escutti; Eyzaguirre; Contreras; Sanchez, R.; Navarro; Toro; Rojas; Ramirez; Landa, Tobar; Sanchez, L.

RUSSIA 1
Yachine; Tchokelli; Ostrovski; Voronin; Maslenkin; Netto; Chislenko; Ivanov; Ponedelnik; Mamikin; Meshki.

SCORERS

Sanchez, L.; Rojas for Chile
Chislenko for Russia
HT 2/1

RANCAGUA

CZECHOSLOVAKIA 1
Schroiff; Lala; Novak; Pluskal; Popluhar; Masopust; Pospichal; Scherer; Kvasniak; Kadraba; Jelinek.

HUNGARY 0
Groscis; Matrai; Sarosi; Solymosi; Meszoly; Sipos; Sandor; Rakosi; Albert; Tichy; Fenyvesi.

SCORER

Scherer for Czechoslovakia
HT 1/0

SEMI-FINALS
SANTIAGO

BRAZIL 4
Gilmar; Santos, D.; Mauro; Zozimo; Santos, N.; Zito; Didi; Garrincha; Vavà; Amarildo; Zagalo.

CHILE 2
Escutti; Eyzaguirre; Contreras; Sanchez, R.; Rodriguez; Toro; Rojas; Ramirez; Landa; Tobar; Sanchez, L.

SCORERS

Garrincha (2), Vavà (2), for Brazil
Toro, Sanchez, L. (penalty) for Chile
HT 2/1

VINA DEL MAR

CZECHOSLOVAKIA 3
Schroiff; Lala; Novak; Pluskal; Popluhar; Masopust; Pospichal; Scherer; Kvasniak; Kadraba; Jelinek.

YUGOSLAVIA 1
Soskic; Durkovic; Jusufi; Radakovic; Markovic; Popovic; Sujakovic; Sekularac; Jerkovic; Galic; Skoblar.

SCORERS

Kadraba, Scherer (2), for Czechoslovakia
Jerkovic for Yugoslavia
HT 0/0

THIRD PLACE MATCH
SANTIAGO

CHILE 1
Godoy; Eyzaguirre; Cruz; Sanchez, R.; Rodriguez; Toro; Rojas; Ramirez; Campos; Tobar; Sanchez, L.

YUGOSLAVIA 0
Soskic; Durkovic; Svinjarevic; Radakovic; Markovic; Popovic; Kovacevic; Sekularac; Jerkovic; Galic; Skoblar.

SCORER

Rojas for Chile
HT 0/0

FINAL
SANTIAGO

BRAZIL 3
Gilmar; Santos, D.;
Mauro; Zozimo; Santos,
N.; Zito; Didi;
Garrincha; Vavà;
Amarildo; Zagalo.

CZECHOSLOVAKIA 1
Schroiff; Tichy; Novak;
Pluskal; Popluhar;
Masopust; Pospichal;
Scherer; Kvasniak;
Kadraba; Jelinek.

SCORERS
Amarildo, Zito, Vavà for Brazil
Masopust for Czechoslovakia
HT 1/1

ENGLAND 1966
GROUP 1

England 0, Uruguay 0 (HT 0/0)
France 1, Mexico 1 (HT 0/0)
Uruguay 2, France 1 (HT 2/1)
England 2, Mexico 0 (HT 1/0)
Uruguay 0, Mexico 0 (HT 0/0)
England 2, France 0 (HT 1/0)

	P	W	D	L	GOALS F	A	Pts
England	3	2	1	0	4	0	5
Uruguay	3	1	2	0	2	1	4
Mexico	3	0	2	1	1	3	2
France	3	0	1	2	2	5	1

GROUP 2

West Germany 5, Switzerland 0 (HT 3/0)
Argentina 2, Spain 1 (HT 0/0)
Spain 2, Switzerland 1 (HT 0/1)
Argentina 0, West Germany 0 (HT 0/0)
Argentina 2, Switzerland 0 (HT 0/0)
West Germany 2, Spain 1 (HT 1/1)

	P	W	D	L	GOALS F	A	Pts
West Germany	3	2	1	0	7	1	5
Argentina	3	2	1	0	4	1	5
Spain	3	1	0	2	4	5	2
Switzerland	3	0	0	3	1	9	0

GROUP 3

Brazil 2, Bulgaria 0 (HT 1/0)
Portugal 3, Hungary 1 (HT 1/0)
Hungary 3, Brazil 1 (HT 1/1)
Portugal 3, Bulgaria 0 (HT 2/0)
Portugal 3, Brazil 1 (HT 2/0)
Hungary 3, Bulgaria 1 (HT 2/1)

	P	W	D	L	GOALS F	A	Pts
Portugal	3	3	0	0	9	2	6
Hungary	3	2	0	1	7	5	4
Brazil	3	1	0	2	4	6	2
Bulgaria	3	0	0	3	1	8	0

GROUP 4

Russia 3, North Korea 0 (HT 2/0)
Italy 2, Chile 0 (HT 1/0)
Chile 1, North Korea 1 (HT 1/0)
Russia 1, Italy 0 (HT 0/0)
North Korea 1, Italy 0 (HT 1/0)
Russia 2, Chile 1 (HT 1/1)

	P	W	D	L	GOALS F	A	Pts
Russia	3	3	0	0	6	1	6
North Korea	3	1	1	1	2	4	3
Italy	3	1	0	2	2	2	2
Chile	3	0	1	2	2	5	1

QUARTER-FINALS
WEMBLEY

ENGLAND 1
Banks; Cohen; Wilson;
Stiles; Charlton, J.;
Moore; Ball; Hurst;
Charlton, R.; Hunt, Peters.

ARGENTINA 0
Roma; Ferreiro; Perfumo;
Albrecht; Marzolini;
Gonzalez; Rattin; Onega;
Solari; Artime; Mas.

SCORER
Hurst for England
HT 0/0

SHEFFIELD

WEST GERMANY 4
Tilkowski; Hottges;
Weber; Schulz;
Schnellinger;
Beckenbauer; Haller;
Overath; Seeler; Held;
Emmerich.

URUGUAY 0
Mazurkiewicz; Troche;
Ubinas; Goncalves;
Manicera; Caetano; Salva;
Rocha; Silva; Cortes;
Perez.

SCORERS
Held, Beckenbauer, Seeler, Haller for West Germany
HT 1/0

EVERTON

PORTUGAL 5
José Pereira; Morais;
Baptista; Vicente;
Hilario; Graca; Coluna;
José Augusto; Eusebio;
Torres; Simoes.

NORTH KOREA 3
Li Chan Myung; Rim
Yung Sum; Shin Yung
Kyoo; Ha Jung Won; O
Yoon Kyung; Pak Seung
Jin; Jon Seung Hwi; Han
Bong Jin; Pak Doo Ik; Li
Dong Woon; Yang Sung
Kook.

SCORERS

Eusebio (4) (2 penalties), José Augusto for Portugal
Pak Seung Jin, Yang Sung Kook, Li Dong Woon for
North Korea
HT 2/3

SUNDERLAND

RUSSIA 2
Yachine; Ponomarev;
Chesternijev; Voronin;
Danilov; Sabo;
Khusainov; Chislenko;
Banichevski; Malafeev;
Porkujan.

HUNGARY 1
Gelei; Matrai; Kaposzta;
Meszoly; Sipos; Szepesi;
Nagy; Albert; Rakosi;
Bene; Farkas.

SCORERS

Chislenko, Porkujan for Russia
Bene for Hungary
HT 1/0

SEMI-FINALS
EVERTON

WEST GERMANY 2
Tilkowski; Hottges;
Weber; Schulz;
Schnellinger;
Beckenbauer; Haller;
Overath; Seeler; Held;
Emmerich.

RUSSIA 1
Yachine; Ponomarev;
Chesternijev; Voronin;
Danilov; Sabo;
Khusainov; Chislenko;
Banichevski; Malafeev;
Porkujan.

SCORERS

Haller, Beckenbauer for Germany
Porkujan for Russia
HT 1/0

WEMBLEY

ENGLAND 2
Banks; Cohen; Wilson;
Stiles; Charlton, J.;
Moore; Ball; Hurst;
Charlton, R.; Hunt; Peters.

PORTUGAL 1
José Pereira; Festa;
Baptista; José Carlos;
Hilario; Graca; Coluna;
José Augusto; Eusebio;
Torres; Simoes.

SCORERS

Charlton, R. (2) for England
Eusebio (penalty) for Portugal
HT 1/0

THIRD PLACE MATCH
WEMBLEY

PORTUGAL 2
José Pereira; Festa;
Baptista; José Carlos;

RUSSIA 1
Yachine; Ponomarev;
Khurtsilava; Korneev;

Hilario; Graca; Coluna;
José Augusto; Eusebio;
Torres; Simoes.

Danilov; Voronin;
Sichinava; Metreveli;
Malafeev; Banichevski;
Serebrianikov.

SCORERS

Eusebio (penalty), Torres for Portugal
Malafeev for Russia
HT 1/1

FINAL
WEMBLEY

ENGLAND 4
(after extra time)
Banks; Cohen; Wilson;
Stiles; Charlton, J.; Moore;
Ball; Hurst; Hunt;
Charlton, R.; Peters.

WEST GERMANY 2
Tilkowski; Hottges;
Schulz; Weber;
Schnellinger; Haller;
Beckenbauer; Overath;
Seeler; Held; Emmerich.

SCORERS

Hurst (3), Peters for England
Haller, Weber for Germany
HT 1/1

MEXICO 1970
GROUP 1

Mexico 0, Russia 0 (HT 0/0)
Belgium 3, El Salvador 0 (HT 1/0)
Russia 4, Belgium 1 (HT 1/0)
Mexico 4, El Salvador 0 (HT 1/0)
Russia 2, El Salvador 0 (HT 0/0)
Mexico 1, Belgium 0 (HT 1/0)

		GOALS					
	P	W	D	L	F	A	Pts
Russia	3	2	1	0	6	1	5
Mexico	3	2	1	0	5	0	5
Belgium	3	1	0	2	4	5	2
El Salvador	3	0	0	3	0	9	0

GROUP 2

Uruguay 2, Israel 0 (HT 1/0)
Italy 1, Sweden 0 (HT 1/0)
Uruguay 0, Italy 0 (HT 0/0)
Sweden 1, Israel 1 (HT 0/0)
Sweden 1, Uruguay 0 (HT 0/0)
Italy 0, Israel 0 (HT 0/0)

		GOALS					
	P	W	D	L	F	A	Pts
Italy	3	1	2	0	1	0	4
Uruguay	3	1	1	1	2	1	3
Sweden	3	1	1	1	2	2	3
Israel	3	0	2	1	1	3	2

GROUP 3

England 1, Romania 0 (HT 0/0)
Brazil 4, Czechoslovakia 1 (HT 1/1)
Romania 2, Czechoslovakia 1 (HT 0/1)
Brazil 1, England 0 (HT 0/0)
Brazil 3, Romania 2 (HT 2/1)
England 1, Czechoslovakia 0 (HT 0/0)

		GOALS					
	P	W	D	L	F	A	Pts
Brazil	3	3	0	0	8	3	6
England	3	2	0	1	2	1	4
Romania	3	1	0	2	4	5	2
Czechoslovakia	3	0	0	3	2	7	0

GROUP 4

Peru 3, Bulgaria 2 (HT 0/1)
West Germany 2, Morocco 1 (HT 0/1)
Peru 3, Morocco 0 (HT 0/0)
West Germany 5, Bulgaria 2 (HT 2/1)
West Germany 3, Peru 1 (HT 3/1)
Morocco 1, Bulgaria 1 (HT 1/0)

		GOALS					
	P	W	D	L	F	A	Pts
West Germany	3	3	0	0	10	4	6
Peru	3	2	0	1	7	5	4
Bulgaria	3	0	1	2	5	9	1
Morocco	3	0	1	2	2	6	1

QUARTER-FINALS
LEON

WEST GERMANY 3   **ENGLAND 2**
(after extra time)
Maier; Schnellinger;   Bonetti; Newton; Cooper;
Vogts; Hottges (Schulz);   Mullery; Labone; Moore;
Beckenbauer; Overath;   Lee; Ball; Hurst;
Seeler; Libuda;   Charlton (Bell); Peters

(Grabowski); Muller;   (Hunter).
Loehr.

SCORERS

Beckenbauer, Seeler, Muller for West Germany
Mullery, Peters for England
HT 0/1

GUADALAJARA

BRAZIL 4   **PERU 2**
Felix; Carlos Alberto;   Rubinos; Campos;
Brito; Piazza; Marco   Fernandez; Chumpitaz;
Antonio; Clodoaldo;   Fuentes; Mifflin; Challe;
Gerson (Paulo Cesar);   Baylon (Sotil); Perico Leon
Jairzinho (Roberto);   (Eladio Reyes), Cubillas;
Tostao; Pelé; Rivelino.   Gallardo.

SCORERS

Rivelino, Tostao (2), Jairzinho for Brazil
Gallardo, Cubillas for Peru
HT 2/1

TOLUCA

ITALY 4   **MEXICO 1**
Albertosi; Burgnich; Cera;   Calderon; Vantolra; Pena;
Rosato; Facchetti;   Guzman; Perez; Gonzalez;
Bertini; Mazzola (Rivera);   (Borja); Pulido; Munguia
De Sisti; Domenghini   (Diaz); Valdivia; Fragoso;
(Gori); Boninsegna; Riva.   Padilla.

SCORERS

Domenghini, Riva (2), Rivera for Italy
Gonzalez for Mexico
HT 1/1

MEXICO CITY

URUGUAY 1   **RUSSIA 0**
(after extra time)
Mazurkiewicz; Ubinas;   Kavazashvili;
Ancheta; Matosas; Mujica;   Dzodzuashvili; Afonin;
Maneiro; Cortes;   Khurtsilava (Logofet);
Montero Castillo; Cubilla;   Chesternijev; Muntijan;
Fontes (Gomez); Morales   Asatiani (Kiselev);
(Esparrago).   Kaplichni; Evriuzhkinzin;
  Bychevetz; Khmelnitzki.

SCORER

Esparrago for Uruguay
HT 0/0

SEMI-FINALS
MEXICO CITY

ITALY 4   **WEST GERMANY 3**
(after extra time)
Albertosi; Cera;   Maier; Schnellinger;
Burgnich; Rosato   Vogts; Schulz;
(Poletti); Facchetti;   Beckenbauer; Patzke
Domenghini; Mazzola   (Held); Seeler; Overath;
(Rivera); De Sisti;   Grabowski; Muller; Loehr
Boninsegna; Riva.   (Libuda).

SCORERS

Boninsegna, Burgnich, Riva, Rivera for Italy
Schnellinger, Muller (2) for West Germany
HT 1/0

GUADALAJARA

BRAZIL 3
Felix; Carlos; Alberto;
Brito; Piazza; Everaldo;
Clodoaldo; Gerson;
Jairzinho; Tostao; Pelé;
Rivelino.

URUGUAY 1
Mazurkiewicz; Ubinas;
Ancheta; Matosas; Mujica;
Montero Castillo; Cortes;
Fontes; Cubilla; Maneiro
(Esparrago); Morales.

SCORERS

Clodoaldo, Jairzinho, Rivelino for Brazil
Cubilla for Uruguay
HT 1/1

THIRD PLACE MATCH
MEXICO CITY

WEST GERMANY 1
Wolter; Schnellinger
(Lorenz); Patzke; Fichtel;
Weber; Vogts; Seeler;
Overath; Libuda (Loehr);
Muller; Held.

URUGUAY 0
Mazurkiewicz; Ubinas;
Ancheta; Matosas; Mujica;
Montero Castillo; Cortes;
Fontes (Sandoval);
Cubilla; Maneiro
(Esparrago); Morales.

SCORER

Overath for West Germany
HT 1/0

FINAL
MEXICO CITY

BRAZIL 4
Felix; Carlos Alberto;
Brito; Piazza; Everaldo;
Clodoaldo; Gerson;
Jairzinho; Tostao; Pelé;
Rivelino.

ITALY 1
Albertosi; Cera;
Burgnich; Bertini
(Juliano); Rosato;
Facchetti; Domenghini;
Mazzola; De Sisti;
Boninsegna (Rivera); Riva.

SCORERS

Pelé, Gerson, Jairzinho, Carlos Alberto for Brazil
Boninsegna for Italy
HT 1/1

WEST GERMANY 1974
POOL 1

West Germany 1, Chile 0 (HT 1/0)
East Germany 2, Australia 0 (HT 0/0)

Chile 1, East Germany 1 (HT 0/0)
Australia 0, West Germany 3 (HT 0/2)
Australia 0, Chile 0 (HT 0/0)
East Germany 1, West Germany 0 (HT 0/0)

		P	W	D	L	GOALS F	A	Pts
East Germany		3	2	1	0	4	1	5
West Germany		3	2	0	1	4	1	4
Chile		3	0	2	1	1	2	2
Australia		3	0	1	2	0	5	1

POOL 2

Brazil 0, Yugoslavia 0 (HT 0/0)
Zaire 0, Scotland 2 (HT 0/2)
Yugoslavia 9, Zaire 0 (HT 6/0)
Scotland 0, Brazil 0 (HT 0/0)
Scotland 1, Yugoslavia 1 (HT 0/0)
Zaire 0, Brazil 3 (HT 0/1)

	P	W	D	L	GOALS F	A	Pts
Yugoslavia	3	1	2	0	10	1	4
Brazil	3	1	2	0	3	0	4
Scotland	3	1	2	0	3	1	4
Zaire	3	0	0	3	0	14	0

POOL 3

Uruguay 0, Holland 2 (HT 0/1)
Sweden 0, Bulgaria 0 (HT 0/0)
Holland 0, Sweden 0 (HT 0/0)
Bulgaria 1, Uruguay 1 (HT 0/0)
Bulgaria 1, Holland 4 (HT 0/2)
Sweden 3, Uruguay 0 (HT 0/0)

	P	W	D	L	GOALS F	A	Pts
Holland	3	2	1	0	6	1	5
Sweden	3	1	2	0	3	0	4
Bulgaria	3	0	2	1	2	5	2
Uruguay	3	0	1	2	1	6	1

POOL 4

Italy 3, Haiti 1 (HT 0/0)
Poland 3, Argentina 2 (HT 2/0)
Haiti 0, Poland 7 (HT 0/5)
Argentina 1, Italy 1 (HT 1/1)
Argentina 4, Haiti 1 (HT 2/0)
Poland 2, Italy 1 (HT 2/0)

	P	W	D	L	GOALS F	A	Pts
Poland	3	3	0	0	12	3	6
Argentina	3	1	1	1	7	5	3
Italy	3	1	1	1	5	4	3
Haiti	3	0	0	3	2	14	0

GROUP A
HANNOVER

BRAZIL 1
Leao; Ze Maria;
Luiz Pereira; Marinho (S);

EAST GERMANY 0
Croy; Kurbjuweit;
Bransch; Weise; Streich;

Marinho (F); Paulo César "Carpegiani"; Rivelino; Dirceu; Valdomino; Jairzinho; Paulo Cesar (L).

Waetzlich; Lauck (Loewe); Sparwasser; Hannann (Irmscher); Kische; Hoffmann.

SCORER

Rivelino for Brazil
HT 0/0

GELSENKIRCHEN

HOLLAND 4
Hoan; van Hanegem; Jansen; Jongbloed; Krol; Neeskens; Cruyff; Riesenbrink; Rep; Rijsbergen; Suurbier (Israel)

ARGENTINA 0
Carnevali; Pierfumo; Sa; Wolff (Gloria); Telch; Heredia; Balbuena; Yazalde; Ayola; Squeo; Houseman (Kempes)

SCORERS

Cruyff, Krol, Rep, Cruyff for Holland
HT 2/0

GELSENKIRCHEN

EAST GERMANY 0
Croy; Kurbjeuveit; Bransch; Weise; Schnuphose; Pommerenke; Loewe (Ducke); Lauck (Kreische); Sparwasser; Kische; Hoffmann.

HOLLAND 2
Jongbloed; Suurbier; Hann; Rysbergen; Krol; Jansen; Neeskens; van Hanegem; Rep; Cruyff; Rensenbrink.

SCORERS

Neeskens, Rensenbrink for Holland
HT 0/1

HANNOVER

ARGENTINA 1
Carnevali; Claria; Heredia; Bargas; Pedro Sa (Carrascosa); Brindisi; Squeo; Babington; Balbuera; Ayala; Kempes (Houseman).

BRAZIL 2
Laeo; Ze Maria; Pereira; Marinho; Marinho (F); P. Cesar (Car); Rivelino; Dirceu; Valdomiro; Jairzinho; P. Cesar (L).

SCORERS

Rivelino, Jairzinho for Brazil
Brindisi for Argentina
HT 1/1

GELENSENKIRCHEN

ARGENTINA 1
Follol; Wolff; Heredia; Bargas; Carrascosa; Brindisi; Telch; Babington; Houseman; Ayala; Kempes.

EAST GERMANY 1
Croy; Kurbjurveit; Bransch; Weise; Schnuphase; Pommerenka; Loewe (Vogel); Streich (Ducke); Sparwasse; Kische; Hoffmann.

SCORERS

Streich for East Germany
Houseman for Argentina
HT 1/1

DORTMUND

HOLLAND 2
Jongbloed; Suurbier; Krol;

BRAZIL 0
Laeo; Luiz Pereira;

Neeskens (Israel); Hann; Rijsbergen; Rep; van Hanegem; Cruyff; Jansen; Riesenbrink (de Jong).

Marinho (S); Ze Maria; Marinho (F);|Carpegiani; Jairzinho; Rivelino; P. Cesar (Mirandinha); Valdomiro; Dirceu.

SCORERS

Neeskens, Cruyff for Holland
HT 0/0

		P	W	D	L	F	A	Pts
						GOALS		
Holland		3	3	0	0	8	0	6
Brazil		3	2	0	1	3	3	4
East Germany		3	0	1	2	1	4	1
Argentina		3	0	1	2	2	7	1

GROUP B
DUSSELDORF

YUGOSLAVIA 0
Marie; Buljan; Habriabdic; Murinic; Katalinski; Oblak (Petkovic); Popivoda; Acimovic; Surjak; Karasi; Dzajic (Jerkovic).

WEST GERMANY 2
Maier; Vogts; Breitner; Schwarzenbeck; Beckenbauer; Bonhof; Wimmer (Hoeness); Hoelbrenbien (Flohe); Overath; Müller; Hierzog.

SCORERS

Breitner, Müller for West Germany
HT 0/1

STUTTGART

SWEDEN 0
Hellström; Andersson (Augustsson); Grip; Karlsson; Nordqvist; Larsson; Torstensson; Tapper (Ahlaström); Edström; Grahn; Sandberg.

POLAND 1
Tomaszewski; Gut; Gorgon; Szymanowski; Zmuda; Kasperczak; Dienya; Massczyk; Lato; Szarmach (Kmiecik); Gadocha.

SCORER

Lato for Poland
HT 0/0

DUSSELDORF

WEST GERMANY 4
Maier; Vogts; Breitner; Schwarzenbeck; Beckenbauer; Bonhof; Hoeness; Hoelzenbien (Flohe); Overath; Müller; Hierzog (Grabowski).

SWEDEN 2
Hellström; Olsson; Augustsson; Karlsson; Nordqvist; Larsson (Ejderstedt); Torstensson; Tapper; Edström; Grahn; Sandberg.

SCORERS

Overath, Bonhof, Grabowski, Hoeness (penalty) for West Germany
Edström, Sandberg for Sweden
HT 0/1

FRANKFURT

POLAND 2
Tomaszewski (Domarski); Szymanowski; Gorgon; Zmuda; Musial;

YUGOSLAVIA 1
Maric; Buljan; Hadziabclic; Bogicevec; Katalinski; Oblak; (Jierkovic);

Kasperczak; Massezyk; Dieyna; Lato; Szarmach; (Cmikienwicz); Gadoeha.

Pietkovic (Petrovic); Karasi; Bajeirc; Acimovic; Surjak.

SCORERS

Dieyna (penalty), Lato for Poland
Karasi for Yugoslavia
HT 1/1

FRANKFURT

POLAND 0
Tomaszewski;
Szymanowski; Gorgon;
Zmuda; Musial;
Casperczak (Cmikiewicz);
Dieyna; Maszezyk
(Kmiecik); Lato;
Domarski; Gadocha.

WEST GERMANY 1
Maier; Vogts; Breitner;
Schwarcenbeck;
Beckenbauer; Bonhof;
Hoeness; Grabowski;
Overath; Müller;
Hoelzenbien.

SCORER

Müller for West Germany
HT 0/0

DUSSELDORF

SWEDEN 2
Hellström; Olsson;
Augustsson; Karlsson;
Nordqvist; Piersson;
Torsterisson; Tapper;
Edström; Grahn;
Sandberg.

YUGOSLAVIA 1
Maric; Buljan; Hadziabdic;
Pavlovic (Pieruzovic);
Katalinski; Bogicevic;
Petrovic (Karasi);
Jierkovic; Surjak;
Acimovic; Dzajic.

SCORERS

Surjak for Yugoslavia
Edström, Torstensson for Sweden
HT 1/1

GOALS

	P	W	D	L	F	A	Pts
West Germany	3	3	0	0	7	2	6
Poland	3	2	0	1	3	2	4
Sweden	3	1	0	2	4	6	2
Yugoslavia	3	0	0	3	2	6	0

3rd/4th PLACE MATCH
MUNICH

BRAZIL 0
Leao; Ze Maria; Mario
Marinho; Alfredo;
Francisco Marinho;
Rivelino; P, Cesar
"Carpegiani"; Ademir
(Mirandinha); Valdomiro;
Jairzinho; Dirceau.

POLAND 1
Tomaszewski;
Szymanowski; Gorgon;
Zmuda; Musial;
Casperozak (Cmikiewicz);
Maszeyk; Dieyna; Lato;
Szarmach (Kapka);
Gadocha.

SCORER

Lato for Poland
HT 0/0

FINAL
MUNICH

HOLLAND 1
Jongbloed; Suurbier;

WEST GERMANY 2
Maier; Vogts;

Rysbergen (de Jong); Haan; Krol; Jansen; van Hanegam; Neeskens; Rep; Cruyff; Riensenbrink; (van de Kerkhof).

Schwarzenbeck;
Beckenbauer; Breitner;
Hoeness; Bonhof; Overath;
Grabowski; Müller;
Hoelzanbein.

SCORERS

Neeskens (penalty) for Holland
Breitner (penalty), Müller for West Germany
HT 1/2

WORLD CUP 1974
FINAL TABLES
GROUP 1

	P	W	D	L	F	A	Pts
East Germany	3	2	1	0	4	1	5
West Germany	3	2	0	1	4	1	4
Chile	3	0	2	1	1	2	2
Australia	3	0	1	2	0	5	1

GROUP 2

	P	W	D	L	F	A	Pts
Yugoslavia	3	1	2	0	10	1	4
Brazil	3	1	2	0	3	0	4
Scotland	3	1	2	0	3	1	4
Zaire	3	0	0	3	0	14	0

GROUP 3

	P	W	D	L	F	A	Pts
Holland	3	2	1	0	6	1	5
Sweden	3	1	2	0	3	0	4
Bulgaria	3	0	2	1	2	5	2
Uruguay	3	0	1	2	1	6	1

GROUP 4

	P	W	D	L	F	A	Pts
Poland	3	3	0	0	12	3	6
Argentina	3	1	1	1	7	5	3
Italy	3	1	1	1	5	4	3
Haiti	3	0	0	3	2	14	0

SEMI-FINAL GROUPS
GROUP A

	P	W	D	L	F	A	Pts
Holland	3	3	0	0	8	0	6
Brazil	3	2	0	1	3	3	4
East Germany	3	0	1	2	1	4	1
Argentina	3	0	1	2	2	7	1

GROUP B

	P	W	D	L	F	A	Pts
West Germany	3	3	0	0	7	2	6
Poland	3	2	0	1	3	2	4
Sweden	3	1	0	2	4	6	2
Yugoslavia	3	0	0	3	2	6	0

THIRD PLACE MATCH

Poland 1, Brazil 0

FINAL

West Germany 2, Holland 1

STATISTICS OF THE 10 WORLD CUP FINAL TOURNAMENTS

In the 10 World Cup Final Tournaments to date, 45 national teams have taken part. A total of 270 matches were played, 226 of which were won or lost outright and only 44 ended in draws. A total of 947 goals were scored, which gives an average of 3.5 goals per match.

	P	M	W	D	L	Goals	Pts
1 Brazil	10	45	29	7	9	109:53	65
2 Germany FR	8	41	27	5	9	100:63	59
3 Italy	8	29	16	5	8	53:34	37
4 Uruguay	7	29	14	5	10	57:39	33
5 Hungary	6	23	13	2	8	70:34	28
6 Sweden	6	25	11	5	9	47:43	27
7 England	6	24	10	6	8	34:28	26
8 Yugoslavia	6	25	10	5	10	45:34	25
9 USSR	4	19	10	3	6	30:21	23
10 Argentina	6	22	9	4	9	40:39	22
11 CSSR	6	22	8	3	11	32:36	19
12 France	6	17	7	1	9	38:33	15
13 Chile	5	17	6	3	8	18:22	15
14 Spain	4	15	6	2	7	20:23	14
15 Austria	3	12	6	1	5	26:26	13
16 Poland	2	8	6	1	2	21:11	12
17 Switzerland	6	18	5	2	11	28:44	12
18 Netherlands	3	9	5	1	3	17:9	11
19 Portugal	1	6	5	0	1	17:8	10
20 Mexico	7	21	3	4	14	19:50	10
21 German DR	1	6	2	2	2	5:5	6
22 Paraguay	3	7	2	2	3	12:19	6
23 USA	3	7	3	0	4	12:21	6
24 Wales	1	5	1	3	1	4:4	5
25 Ireland North	1	5	2	1	2	5:9	5
26 Rumania	4	8	2	1	5	12:17	5
27 Scotland	3	8	1	3	4	7:15	5
28 Peru	2	6	2	0	4	10:13	4
29 Bulgaria	4	12	0	4	8	9:29	4
30 Korea North	1	4	1	1	2	5:9	3
31 Cuba	1	3	1	1	1	5:12	3
32 Belgium	5	9	1	1	7	12:25	3
33 Turkey	1	3	1	0	2	10:11	2
34 Israel	1	3	0	2	1	1:3	2
35 Bolivia	2	4	1	0	3	5:18	2
36 Morocco	1	3	0	1	2	2:6	1
37 Australia	1	3	0	1	2	0:5	1
38 Colombia	1	3	0	1	2	5:11	1
39 Norway	1	1	0	0	1	1:2	0
40 Egypt AR	1	1	0	0	1	2:4	0
41 Dutch East Indies	1	1	0	0	1	0:6	0
42 El Salvador	1	3	0	0	3	0:9	0
43 Haiti	1	3	0	0	3	2:14	0
44 Zaire	1	3	0	0	3	0:14	0
45 Korea South	1	2	0	0	2	0:16	0
	153	540	226	88	226	947:947	540

As **World Champion** on the list of winners, we find:
Three times: Brazil (1958, 1962, 1970)
Twice: Uruguay (1930, 1950) Italy (1934, 1938)
Germany FR (1954, 1974)
Once: England (1966)

It is curious to note that, although there were only five different World Champions, ten **runners-up** have been entered on the list, namely:

1930 – Argentina, 1934 – Czechoslovakia, 1938 – Hungary, 1950 – Brazil, 1954 – Hungary, 1958 – Sweden, 1962 – Czechoslovakia, 1966 – Germany FR, 1970 – Italy, 1974 – Netherlands.

In **third place** we find:
Twice: Germany (FR (1934, 1970)
Once: Yugoslavia (1930), Brazil (1938), Sweden (1950), Austria (1954), France (1958), Chile (1962), Portugal (1966), Poland (1974).

In **fourth place** were:
Twice: Uruguay (1954, 1970)
Once: USA (1930), Austria (1934), Sweden (1938), Spain (1950), Germany FR (1958), Yugoslavia (1962), USSR (1966), Brazil (1974).

Chapter Two

THE SUPERSTARS

The gods rarely smile. It would seem that almost every time they decide to bless some mere mortal with greatness, he repays them with a life of chaotic blunders, tantrums, wasted talent and self-destruction.

We have grown accustomed to hearing tales of great writers, poets, musicians and scientists whose individual genius either drove them to near-madness or provided those with weak characters with an excuse for a highly eccentric way of life. Modern sporting prodigies are, with rare exceptions, no different. Too many truly gifted sportsmen have frittered away their talent; this applies especially to football, where potential greatness has been recognised, worshipped and mourned all in the space of a handful of frustrating years.

Small wonder, then, that the gods find it difficult to be patient with men. In fact, possibly the only reason they resist the temptation to shower us with bolts of lightning is that there are a small number of men and women who have accepted their selection for a touch of greatness, appreciated their divine gift and developed their talent for the benefit of mankind. They are what we now call 'superstars', and it is with football's rare and talented superstars that we are concerned in this chapter.

'Kaiser Franz'

The last time the gods smiled on the football world was on 7 July, 1974. Along with the rest of the world, they watched a tall, dark arrogant and aristocratic young Bavarian stride up to receive the coveted gold statuette that is the World Cup. Franz Anton Beckenbauer, one of modern football's superstars, turned to posterity and lifted the trophy above his head – a natural and understandable gesture which whipped up the mounting fervour of the Munich crowd. It seemed fitting that Beckenbauer should be the man to hold the greatest prize in football, and hold it on his native soil, in the town of his birth and in front of his kinfolk, many of whom no doubt had watched him grow from boy to man to master.

Like some Arthurian crusading knight, Beckenbauer travelled the world in search of that moment. Three World Cup competitions, thousands of miles and eight years later, he clutched that which he had sought for so long, absorbed its significance for a few precious seconds and then gave it over to his countrymen.

In so many ways, Beckenbauer was destined to be the winning captain on the day of the World Cup final. Holland, West Germany's opponents, had everything on their side – a wealth of brilliant

Below: Cruyff hurdles a Belgian defender in a 1977 World Cup qualifying match.
Facing page left: A battered Pele limps from the pitch after Portugal had ended Brazil's hopes in 1966.
Facing page right: Beckenbauer victorious in 1974.

Too many truly gifted sportsmen have frittered away their talent

individual skills, welded together into one whole unit which foxed everyone by playing, not to a series of set-patterns, but purely off the cuff. This total football thrilled the world. And when a first minute penalty was awarded against them, West Germany appeared to be in trouble. Beckenbauer, however, forced destiny's hand. He willed his team to succeed and willed himself to collect the gold trophy on behalf of his country.

And so the gods saw their prodigy fulfil the last possible ambition within his field – every major honour a footballer can win has been won by 'Kaiser' Franz. But the question is, has he won every honour because he is a superstar or has winning every honour made him a superstar? We should look more closely at this question.

Franz Anton Beckenbauer was born in Munich on 11 September, 1945 . . . and born a winner. He showed outstanding skills and all-round ability from an early age and once scored a hundred goals in a season playing centre-forward in a school team. Ironically, Munich 1860 were his great love as a boy. When asked which Munich club he would prefer to join, the young Beckenbauer would indicate that, as far as he was concerned, there was only one club in Munich – 1860. He changed his mind – and the destiny of West German football – after a youth match during which his side took a clobbering from a Munich 1860 defence determined to stem his flow of goals. From that day, Beckenbauer vowed he would play only for city rivals, Bayern Munich. He joined Bayern as a boy and was soon playing for West German schoolboy and youth teams at international level. The evolution of the superstar followed all the normal channels, and by the time he had developed into a full international, West Germany were on their way to England to compete for the 1966 World Cup. Beckenbauer's first World Cup was to light the taper which burned – so slowly but so surely – towards his ultimate triumph eight years later in Munich.

The young and impressionable Beckenbauer had the unenviable task of marking Bobby Charlton in the World Cup final – a job which he did quietly and with a satisfactory measure of success for one so young. For most players, just appearing in a World Cup Final is something dreamed of, day and night. For Beckenbauer, losing that final to England was an agonising experience. His loser's medal meant

Left: West German captain Uwe Seeler congratulates the 'Kaiser' after scoring against England, Leon, 1970.
Facing page: Injured against Italy, 1970 semi-final. Despite having an arm strapped, he played on in one of the finest games ever.

nothing but a reminder of what had to be bettered in the future.

His comments on the 1966 series give some insight to the man and his football philosophy:

'The 1966 World Cup was largely a sterile, aggressive competition with the best players looking over their shoulders all the time in case they were tackled from behind.

'Our big problem was that we were coming to the end of the Inter Milan era, an era which saw the powerful Italian team win two World Club Championships and twice hold the European Cup . . . all achieved on a negative basis of one or two forwards and counter attack from solid defence. Too many club teams and international teams tried to copy this style of play.

'The 1970 World Cup series in Mexico was so different. The skills emerged and the games slowed down. I enjoyed my football in Mexico.

'But the 1966 series just serves to remind me that I have a lot of business interests outside football to make a good living for my wife and family. I do not have to play football to survive.'

Had he not become a footballer, Beckenbauer would probably have gone into assurance. One of his private business interests is, in fact, his own assurance company. But, thank the gods, he did become a footballer, a superstar footballer. What is it about his style and ability that sets him above his fellow professionals?

Beckenbauer's whole approach to football is that of a master of his craft who refuses to be hurried, pushed or influenced by other players. He dictates the pace of a game and he carries the ball smoothly past opponents, often all the way from his deep sweeper's position at the heart of the Bayern defence. His ball control is superb, his accuracy of passing masterful, his reading of a game fascinating in its perception and his ability to organise players around him something to be seen at first-hand.

There are those who say that Beckenbauer is wasted playing in defence. He began his career up front, moved back to midfield and eventually settled in the 'libro' position behind the defence. From there, his perception of the game and his long-passing ability can pin down opponents from an unexpected distance. So often Beckenbauer is the source of all a team's problems, yet they cannot get to him to stifle his ability. Clamping down on Bayern Munich's midfield players often served Beckenbauer's cause because his accuracy from the back could feed the deadly Gerd Muller up front, when key defenders were tied up in midfield.

For West Germany, Beckenbauer mastered all problems on and off the field. A strong-willed natural leader of men, he also proved the springboard for many German attacks – a ploy England failed to foil in Leon in 1970 when he stole up to score the goal which began England's World Cup quarter final downfall. When asked to name the two most memorable games in his career, Beckenbauer side-stepped the 1974 World Cup Final as being 'too easy and too obvious a choice,' and named his two games against

‘ I have a lot of business interests outside football to make a good living for my wife and family. I do not have to play football to survive ’

Franz Beckenbauer

England in 1966 and 1970: 'one victory and one defeat, but two memorable games.' This is a career which includes over a hundred international caps – he is the first West German to reach this milestone – added to which is the fact that he missed only twelve games in ten years of representing his country through three World Cup and European Championships.

Beckenbauer made his debut for West Germany against Sweden in Stockholm in 1965. Significantly, the match was a World Cup qualifier. The young Beckenbauer disguised his nerves from all but the wily and experienced old fox, Uwe Seeler, whose calming influence put the future 'Kaiser' at ease. He has never minced words or pulled punches. He was born to get what he wanted, and his natural arrogance, armed with the knowledge that he was something different from the rest, has caused friction with other players, not all of whom enjoyed the strutting young Bavarian's overbearing manner.

For example, when Beckenbauer was playing for the West German youth team, the manager was Dettmar Cramer, who later became FIFA coach. When Bayern sacked Udo Lattek two years ago, Beckenbauer calmly informed the board: 'I want Cramer!' At that time Cramer held a lucrative post with the United States Soccer Federation. But Beckenbauer refused even to flinch away from his objective . . . and Bayern signed Cramer.

If the final celebrations were heady wine, the build-up to West Germany's success was often bitter vinegar. At one stage they lost the prestige match against East Germany by 1-0 . . . and patience on all sides began to wear thin. But while most of the players muttered their discontentment with the team's overall three-cylinder performances, Beckenbauer took control. His powerful personality and supreme self-confidence did the rest. Nobody will ever know how close the anxious West Germans came to fretting themselves to the edge of disaster. Being the host nation had its advantages, but it also piled extra pressure on the players. Beckenbauer seized the initiative and told manager Helmut Schoen that team changes had to be made. One of his proposed changes shocked both the squad and the nation –

Beckenbauer wanted to leave out his young Bayern team-mate Uli Hoeness. That Beckenbauer wanted it was enough. Hoeness was dropped, West Germany picked up momentum and in course of time Hoeness was brought back to play a major role in the eventual triumph in the final.

Such positive thinking and determined action has no doubt played a big part in helping Beckenbauer build up the fantastic collection of major honours to his name. He has won a World Cup Final, European International Championship, World Club Championship, European Cup (three times), Cup Winners' Cup, and the West German Championship (four times). In addition, he has been West German Player of the Year four times and European Player of the Year twice. Away from football, Beckenbauer and his family live in a sumptuous villa on the outskirts of Munich. His business contracts keep something in the region of £250,000 coming in every year.

But of course nothing is that easy – even when the gods have provided you with a hefty slice of greatness. Surviving in the hectic and often frightening world of the superstar involves playing football politics cleverly and with both eyes wide open, handling the press and public relations men, being seen with the right people at the right time and knowing who not to be seen with at any time.

Now that Beckenbauer has turned his back on Bayern for the even more lucrative spoils of the United States, it is worth examining exactly why he has risked losing his international place for the sake of a transatlantic crossing. When Pele arrived in the United States in 1975, the North American Soccer League required a superstar to attract national interest. They were still selling the credibility and viability of football in the country. But now that football has really taken off in the States, the clubs are no longer looking for ambassadors. They now want to have winning teams. The emphasis is now on quality of play rather than a combination of ability and charisma.

So men such as Beckenbauer are being invited to play in the rapidly developing United States football scene. And with top money available, the top stars are realistic enough to know that with a limited career at their disposal – even the superstar's time runs out quickly – the money being offered them is, to say the least, tempting.

It remains in the hands of the gods as to whether or not we see Franz Beckenbauer in the 1978 World Cup finals in Argentina. West Germany will of course be there as holders, but will 'Kaiser' Franz? Only he knows.

Great Names of the Past

Sadly, there are few players of Beckenbauer's calibre in modern football, but then, over the years, superstars have been few and far between. As one might expect, the World Cup series have produced overnight sensations. But even they were divided into groups of those who had rightfully emerged as

Facing page: Beckenbauer in action for New York Cosmos and **(below)** in the 1977 NASL award winners. In his first season, he managed to maintain his skills on synthetic American pitches.

68

NORTH AMERICAN SOCCER LEAGUE 1977 AWARD WINNERS

COACH OF THE YEAR

RON NEWMAN, *Ft. Lauderdale Strikers*

MOST VALUABLE PLAYER
DEFENDER OF THE YEAR

FRANZ BECKENBAUER, *Cosmos*

TOP SCORER OF THE YEAR
FORWARD OF THE YEAR

STEVE DAVID, *Los Angeles Aztecs*

MIDFIELDER OF THE YEAR

GEORGE BEST, *Los Angeles Aztecs*

GOALKEEPER OF THE YEAR

GORDON BANKS, *Ft. Lauderdale Strikers*

ROOKIE OF THE YEAR

JIM McALISTER, *Seattle Sounders*

> **Surviving in the hectic and often frightening world of the superstar involves playing football politics, being seen with the right people at the right time and knowing who not to be seen with at any time**

superstars and those who went back into obscurity once the spotlight of a World Cup series was taken from them. If we go back to the first World Cup series, the 1930 Uruguay finals, a handful of names still live in the memories of journalists, statistical experts and older managers. Stabile is one name which will last. The Argentinian forward finished the series as top scorer with eight goals, including one in the final when Uruguay won 4-2. He was, perhaps, the first World Cup superstar to carve his name on a little corner of history.

The 1934 World Cup, exploited as a tool for political ends by Mussolini, took place in Italy. There is no doubt that Schiavio was the player of the tournament: he was joint top-scorer with four goals, including the winning goal in the final against Czechoslovakia. Italy won the final 2-1, but Schiavio's ability captured the imagination, and although Conen (Germany) and Nejedly (Czechoslovakia) also scored four goals in the tournament, the Italian was undoubtedly the superstar, especially in the eyes of the fanatical home supporters.

Italy retained their title in 1938, but the undoubted star of the competition was a Brazilian named Leonidas who picked up eight goals as Brazil battled through to third place.

Superstar status in those days, however, was nothing like it is today. The pressures simply did not exist. The media was far less involved in football than it is now and players, no matter how good, were still essentially working men. Today, we talk of Beckenbauer, Pele, Cruyff . . . undoubtedly superstars in their own right. Yet the World Cup series have always produced unforgettable names, great players, majestic performers – Kocsis of Hungary who finished the 1954 series top scorer with eleven goals, Helmut

Rahn who scored two for West Germany in their 3-2 win over Hungary in the final. And Hungary had another player destined to become a legend in his own time – Puskas.

Pele – the Football Ambassador

The 1958 series in Sweden, however, produced the superstar of them all, Pele, the Black Pearl of Brazil. Now here was a superstar with everything. An inexperienced 17-year-old, he scored two goals in the final as Brazil blitzed host nation Sweden 5-2. He missed the 1962 final when Brazil beat Czechoslovakia 3-1, being injured earlier in the tournament, and

when he came to England in 1966 he was brutally kicked out of the competition. This vicious treatment at the hands of desperate opponents almost led to his giving up international football altogether, but in 1970 he roared back, a dazzling star in a dazzling Brazil team which tore apart Italy's negative system in a fantastic final.

The 1974 finals saw the arrival of Cruyff on the world stage. Beckenbauer was already the star attraction in the superstar stakes and players such as Poland's Lato came close to establishing themselves as superstars. To say a player comes close to becoming a superstar is by no means an insult, because the difference, the gap which separates star from super-

star is not so much fine as impossible to define. Superstar status in itself brands a player as something special, someone very different – almost unique. No two superstars ever fall into the same category; you cannot label genius.

So, in order that we understand the anatomy and physiology of the superstar, let us examine, in depth, the careers and life-styles of two more – Pele and Cruyff. In many ways their lives resemble the life of

Franz Beckenbauer, but at the same time their individual genius comes across as the reason for their success.

Pele has very strong views on the subject of natural talent and once shook the entire football world with a short but explosive admission. He said:

'I do not believe there is such a thing as a born footballer. Perhaps you are born with certain skills and talents, but success is no accident. It is hard work, perseverance, learning, studying sacrifice and most of all love of what you are doing or learning to do.'

The immediate reaction is 'If Pele is not a born "natural" then who is?' Yet the man regarded by many as the most complete footballer of all time goes a fair way towards shattering the myth which has grown up in his wake. Pele was born on 23 October, 1940 in Tres Coracoes, Brazil, and lived for most of his childhood in the state of Sao Paulo. A Roman Catholic, he was baptised Edson Arantes do Nascimento – a mouthful by any standards.

His background was poor and like so many Brazilian youngsters he began his career kicking stuffed rags rolled into a makeshift ball around the back streets of his home town. He joined a local club – Noroeste – before being spotted by a famous former international, Waldemar de Brito of Bauro, who played inside right for Brazil in the 1934 World Cup series in Italy. He also holds a record he would rather forget, that of being the first player in the history of the World Cup to miss a penalty – against Spain in Genoa when Brazil lost 3-1.

De Brito sent Pele to Santos where he became a first-team choice at barely sixteen. Pele gave the world an early warning of things to come by scoring eight goals in an important cup tie. Shortly afterwards he made his international debut.

Aged sixteen years and nine months, Pele lined up for Brazil against Argentina in 1957. His last game was against Yugoslavia in 1971. In between – and fourteen years at the very top is a long, long time – Pele played in four World Cup series (1958, 1962, 1966 and 1970) and collected three World Cup winners' medals. He missed the 1962 final, but it is believed that a special medal was struck for him . . . some indication of his importance to Brazilian football.

Match for match, goal for goal, Pele's record is fantastic. His principal honours include 110 full caps, three World Cup medals, two World Club championship medals, three South American Cup winners medals, four Brazilian Cup winners medals and twelve Sao Paulo League championship medals. His international record reads like something out of a boys' comic strip – 96 goals in 110 games, a debut at sixteen and a list of moments which can only be described as magical, moments such as his goals against Sweden in the 1958 final, another against Italy in the 1970 final and the breath-taking attempts at goal from incredible angles and distances throughout his career. Between his first game for Santos on 7 September, 1956 and his last game for them on 2 October, 1974, he scored 1,088 goals in 1,114 games!

Yet for all this, Pele remains the perfect example of the true superstar . . . because of his humility. His

Superstar status brands a player as something special, someone very different —almost unique. No two superstars ever fall into the same category; you cannot label genius

philosophy is staggeringly simple: 'If you become great, do your best to show why you are considered to be so good. If you only reach the level of a reserve player, then show that you are best in that category.'

In 1977, Pele retired from a second career – an incredible feat by a man who looked to have given his all to football prior to his retirement first from international football and subsequently from Santos. The sudden upsurge of soccer in the United States heralded the comeback of the player many people had long since viewed as a legend from the past. New York Cosmos offered him a three-season contract worth £1¾ million plus all taxes paid. As well as playing he would hold coaching clinics, give lectures, make regular television appearances, do advertising commercials and perform many other lucrative functions.

He was an instant hit with Cosmos. He was mobbed every time he showed his face, packed out grounds where previously clubs had been pleased with five-figure gates and gave football in the States the boost it so badly needed. However, Pele learned that football USA-style is rather different to the football he grew up to love. For example, after one of his earlier games for Cosmos during which he scored a fantastic solo goal, the club vice-president came up and complained: 'Pity you scored in one of the commercial breaks!'

Things have changed since then. But Pele showed his superstar calibre by adjusting to every situation as if it were second nature – and that included mastering the English language to the point where he can now give television interviews. Through all the

I do not believe there is such a thing as a born footballer. Perhaps you are born with certain skills and talents, but success is no accident — It is hard work

years of adulation, Pele has remained calm and level-headed. He says:

'I have earned enough to keep my family comfortably off for the rest of our lives. I am involved in many business projects and it is no secret that they have all been a success.

'Sometimes my advisers try to shield me from various situations. But they are often over-cautious. I know what I want and how to handle my life.

'I give a lot of my income to charities, especially to a big hospital in Santos.'

How can one assess the value of a man such as Pele? By his immense natural talent with a football, by his kindness to the poor, by his ability to shut out the world once he is with his family? Perhaps the man's incredible superstar qualities are best summed up by the reaction of former Secretary of State, Dr Henry Kissinger, when he heard of Pele's intended move to Cosmos. He sent a telegram which read:

'Should you decide to sign a contract, I am sure your stay in the United States will contribute substantially to closer ties between Brazil and the United States in the field of sport.'

As if to match the political level of the situation, Brazil's Foreign Minister, Antonio Azeredo da Silveira, contacted Pele and urged him to join the New York club.

On retirement, Pele was not only a great footballer, recognised throughout the world as a superstar, but also the Brazilian sportsman most capable of representing his country wherever he goes. His ability to handle the immense pressures brought on by such a responsibility seals his stamp as a true superstar.

Since his retirement from Brazilian football, Pele's

Facing page top: Maier saves at Cruyff's feet in the 1974 World Cup final. It still remains to be seen whether Cruyff will play in Argentina and give the world a final glimpse of his superlative skills.
Facing page below: Beckenbauer with Helmut Schoen after the 1974 victory and seen later in the dressing room.

crown has wobbled uncertainly on the heads of various pretenders before settling on Roberto Rivelino, the brilliant left-footed midfield genius of Corinthians. Fine player though he is, Rivelino is not another Pele. But he is the most respected and established member of what promises to be Brazil's 1978 World Cup squad. He is the closest we shall get to seeing another Brazilian superstar in this decade. Men such as Paulo Cesar were hailed as the second Pele. But he failed to fulfil great promise and made only one appearance in the 1970 finals. He failed again in 1974, despite possessing great talent.

The closest European football has come to discovering a Pele-type player is Eusebio, the talented African-born Portuguese international who made his name with Benfica. Now 34, Eusebio finished top scorer with nine goals in the 1966 World Cup series in England and played in all four of Benfica's European Cup Finals. One of the most feared strikers in Europe, he resented the endless comparisons with Pele, although he did have great respect for the great Brazilian.

Cruyff — Today's Superstar

Our next subject is the world's current superstar, a man of so many parts that it is difficult to know exactly where to begin. He speaks five languages, puts his family above all else, has a god-given talent to play football yet so far refuses to represent his country in the forthcoming World Cup Finals in Argentina . . . he is the unique Johan Cruyff of Holland.

Johan Cruyff was born in Amsterdam, on 25 April, 1947. From the first day he kicked a football his immense talent was obvious, especially as it was allied with a somewhat fiery temperament and a strong will to succeed. He was born in a poor district where his father worked hard in a greengrocer's shop to ensure that Johan and his brother Henny had a good upbringing.

Cruyff explains:

'I was 13 when my father died and my mother took over running the canteen at the Ajax ground. Henny and I were already playing for the juvenile team and both dreaming of being promoted to the cadets. One by one my dreams came true – cadets, first team, league, European Cup and international recognition.'

Cruyff was the top Dutch goalscorer with 38 goals in his first full season. He was just 18. Superbly skilful, fast, deceptive, two-footed, good in the air, he is capable of uncanny positional play, either up front or in his favourite roaming midfield role where he is almost impossible to mark.

There are three distinct sides to Cruyff – the footballer with skills that are the envy of the world, the businessman with a sharp brain and the backing of a shrewd father-in-law, and the family man, to whom his wife Danny and their children mean more than anything else in life.

Let us first examine the career progress of Cruyff the footballer.

He burst upon the European scene when Ajax reached their first European Cup Final in 1969 and lost 4-1 to AC Milan. That defeat only whetted

Telegram from Dr Henry Kissinger to Pele

'I am sure your stay in the United States will contribute substantially to closer ties between Brazil and the United States'

Cruyff's appetite for success and he stormed back at the hub of a brilliant Ajax team destined to win the European crown three years in a row. He played brilliantly when Ajax beat Greek champions Panathinaikos 2-0 at Wembley in 1971, scored both goals when Ajax beat Inter-Milan 2-0 in 1972 and masterminded the 1-0 1973 triumph over Juventus.

But despite all this success, Cruyff had a problem with his temperament. Once he was suspended from international football for twelve months after being sent off in a match against Czechoslovakia.

Three times named European Footballer of the Year, Cruyff became one of the players of the 1974 World Cup series in West Germany. That he ended with a runners-up medal is still a mystery to all those who recognised Holland's exciting total football as being most deserving of success.

Of the total football pioneered by Holland Cruyff says: 'It was really a psychological thing – we saw the game purely as a team game and tried to help each other in every situation and in every corner of the pitch.'

Franz Beckenbauer came closer to analysing total football when he said:

'It owed more to the element of surprise than to any magic formula. I think the Dutch got away with it for so long because the opposition could not work out what tactics they were facing. It never dawned on them, certainly until it was much too late, that there were no tactics at all . . . just brilliant players with a ball.'

Whatever the root of its success, Holland's style failed to lift the World Cup, as so many experts predicted it would. The final act seemed only a matter of turning up once Holland had swept into the World Cup Final, and when they took a first-minute lead from the penalty spot after Cruyff had been tripped, predictions looked completely on target. On the day, however, Bertie Vogts kept a masterful rein on Cruyff and Holland failed to get into top gear until it was

Above: Cruyff in action for Holland against Bulgaria.
Right: A small reward for his efforts as Cruyff and the Dutch team arrive in Munich for the 1974 final.
Facing page: Attacking for his Spanish club, Barcelona.

Left: Cruyff shoots powerfully during the 1974 series.
Above: Taking on the West German midfield player Bonhof during the 1974 World Cup final in Munich. His generalship on the pitch was the driving force behind the Dutch team's exciting style.

too late. It was that other superstar, Beckenbauer, who coaxed his team to victory.

Now, with Argentina beckoning, Cruyff refuses to go. He says he will not be separated from his family for such a length of time ever again. He adds: 'I doubt whether referees will have the courage to enforce the laws on the South Americans, especially not the Argentinians.'

At the moment, Cruyff is the El Cordobes of football in Spain. He loves the country, enjoys playing for Barcelona, contrary to endless stories that he hates the place, and, if the money is right, will stay there. He cost Barcelona a staggering £922,000 when he joined them in the summer of 1973. His contract

was for three years and expired in May 1976. It cost Barcelona another £220,000 to re-sign him!

Yet in his first three years in Spain, Cruyff collected 19 bookings and was sent off twice. Fifteen bookings and both sendings-off were for arguing with referees. But he sees a key responsibility as captain in representing his team-mates and thus questions every action he considers to be doubtful. For all this, Barcelona and the Spanish fans adore him. One clause

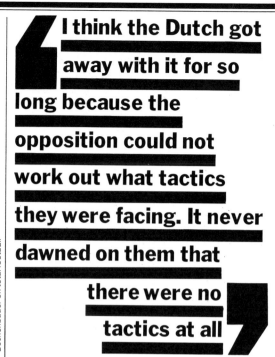

Beckenbauer on total football

in his contract reads to the effect that Barcelona pay his taxes every year – £67,000. That is some measure of their affection for the Dutch genius.

From the day he first went to Ajax and negotiated a contract to his own liking rather than theirs, Cruyff has emerged as a shrewd no-nonsense businessman as well as a footballing superstar. He knows what he is worth and why. He gives what is asked of him. He demands what he is owed in return. His father-in-law, Cor Coster, keeps a close eye on Cruyff's business dealings. As a result the player earns a fortune endorsing various products. Once, when a firm began selling goods under Cruyff's name without his consent, Coster immediately put a copyright on the name 'Cruyff' and showed his razor-sharp brain at its best by also stamping a copyright on the spellings 'Kruyff', 'Cruiff', 'Cruif', 'Kruif', 'Cruijff' and 'Kriyf'.

With such a man at his side, Johan Cruyff knows he has business strength . . . and a unique product, himself. In return for that massive fee and salary paid by Barcelona, he generated increased attendances within four months of his arrival in Spain.

Cruyff turns away from everything, however, when it threatens to interfere with his family life.

He says:

'To me it is important to have a settled home and family, because this is the best antidote to the pressures of the game. It does not matter if I am playing well or badly, the family always comforts me. We never talk about football at home.'

Cruyff lives in a secret hideout up in the Spanish hills, a house surrounded by high walls and a vast amount of woodland. He is willing to plough back a large percentage of his earnings to buy peace and quiet. From Sunday night to Tuesday mornings he disappears from the limelight and the ever-demanding public to be with Danny and the kids.

When he does emerge to face the world, the fact that he is intelligent, charming and speaks five languages is often a rod for his own back. Where many players play dumb when asked a tricky question, Cruyff lines up the journalists and promises each one an interview, wherever possible in their own language, and attempts to answer all questions frankly and openly.

He has become an international personality – another rod for a young and talented back. He was once asked to leave the Royal Garden Hotel, Kensington, because he came to sit with friends wearing a tracksuit. He ended up sitting at the table, calm and joking, wearing a waiter's jacket over his international tracksuit – such is the price of fame and endless recognition.

On top of all this, Cruyff is quick to recognise that if Barcelona have a bad season, he will be made responsible. Without being big-headed he calmly asserts that he is the decisive factor in the team's success. And if success does not come, Cruyff will probably have to go.

Meanwhile, the world waits with bated breath to see if Cruyff will lead the talented Dutchmen to Argentina. They made world news in 1974 when it was revealed that the KNVB, the Royal Netherlands Football Federation, were left with a net £6,750 profit from the gross £533,000 takings. The 22 Dutch players shared £236,000 after receiving £110,000 for qualifying for the World Cup Finals. Too much financial wrangling has tormented Dutch football in recent years and this has certainly detracted from their wonderful skills and ability.

What really worries the world is that Pele is not going to be in Argentina. Beckenbauer may not. Cruyff says there is no way he will travel. Which leaves us with who or what to fill the superstar void?

There will be pretenders, tournament successes and outstanding individuals. But when the gloss wears off, who is going to carry the superstar crown to appease the gods this time?

Argentina's Rene Houseman is certainly a talented and much admired forward. We have already mentioned Roberto Rivelino. West Germany's Gerd Muller would have been a possible candidate, except that he made the point that there is nothing left for a player to achieve once he has scored the winning goal in a World Cup Final. Muller, too, prefers to stay with his family.

Brazil do have some talented youngsters on the way up, among whom the name Zico stands out. He has emerged as a potential star player. But superstar? That remains to be seen. Italy have Giancarlo Antognoni, a skilful midfield star whose idol is none other than Cruyff. And so the list goes on. Every nation represented in Argentina will point to one player, maybe more, whom they see as rightfully entitled to the title 'superstar'. But one doubts if one will be seen. Indeed, the time is ripe for the gods once again to bestow their favours on the head of a young footballer. They may have already done so. For that reason, Argentina 1978 promises to reveal more than simple identity of who will hold the World Cup until 1982.

Chapter Three

THE MEN YOU LOVE TO HATE

Who would want a referee's job? These men are mostly unknown, in general unpraised, and without doubt, underpaid. They deal with players of varying talent committing varying offences – many unseen by partisan crowds. They perform this work with one aim, to help the match progress evenly and entertainingly. Yet it is not unknown, at full-time, for them to be escorted from the pitch by police or armed guards, to be criticized openly by the media, chased and abused by spectators, spat upon, kicked and punched. These men are dedicated to football. Refereeing is their true profession, whatever job they do to earn the bulk of their living. They train rigorously, are on call to travel at a moment's notice and do not ask for anything more in return than a travel allowance and expenses and, when in action, to be considered as the 23rd player on the pitch. When, after years of hard work and honest achievement, they achieve the status of being a member of the FIFA refereeing fraternity and are chosen to officiate at a World Cup tournament, they proudly pack their bags and fly to their destination knowing that whatever happens they carry the tag of 'the men you love to hate.' For in the end, it will be their split-second decisions, right or wrong to the biased eye, which will decide the outcome of the World Cup.

A Historic Decision

The 1966 World Cup Final is into extra-time, with the score standing at two goals apiece. After ten minutes England score. Geoff Hurst smashes the ball against the underside of the crossbar; in a flash it bounces down in the goalmouth and every English player in the goal area leaps with joy and the Wembley crowd roar. In that split second Gottfried Dienst, the Swiss referee who has been officiating the match so well, seems undecided on whether to award the goal

Below: Referee Kreitlin is given a police escort from the pitch after the controversial England-Argentina game in 1966. The match was held up for nine minutes after Rattin was ordered off. Ill-feeling generated by this has rankled until the present day in some quarters, although official goodwill between the two countries has been restored.
Facing page top: FIFA referee blowing for a corner.
Facing page left: Stanley Rous – schoolmaster.
Facing page below: Italian referee Augnes attempts to calm Boninsegna of Juventus.

immediately to England. For a moment, with 22 players on the Wembley turf pausing, he has to decide if the shot is true, whether the ball has crossed the German goal-line. Herr Dienst is immediately surrounded by protesting German players and Wembley and the world become hushed as he rushes over to his Russian linesman, Tofik Bakhramov. There is a brief exchange of gestures – for the language barrier would not have permitted more – and then comes the sight of Herr Dienst pointing to the centre circle. The goal will stand, his decision is final and England are firmly on the way to World Cup glory.

In that brief moment, one man had made a decision that could justify or destroy four years of preparation by FIFA and every competing nation, especially England and West Germany, in this World Championship. A decision *had* to be made; the global audience demanded it. To this day there could be no single person present in that great and famous stadium who would have willingly changed place with Herr Dienst. Bakhramov, the linesman, who had not reached the corner flag and therefore was not in line with the goal, could in this situation only nod his approval and help his senior official. All the political implications laid at Bakhramov's feet must be totally ignored, for here was another dedicated international referee required to 'run the line' in this final, a man who was honoured to be so selected and to carry out his much respected work to the best of his ability.

However, the football world has never been shown conclusive proof that it was or was not a goal, even with all the technical advantages of the eyes of television play-backs, the slow-motion film of many movie cameras and the snapping shutters of a host of still cameras.

One man, out in the middle, in all probability as he moved across to his linesman, made up the minds of the world. It was his job, and he was the only person for whom it was impossible in that now historic moment to say 'I don't know'.

This is the perfect example of a heavily controversial and dramatic decision in the modern game. Once upon a time, when the World Cup was young, refereeing used to be a gentlemanly affair, conducted in a far more friendly atmosphere with the *arbitre* running up and down the pitch in cap and plus-fours. But with the upsurge of nationalistic pride – and prejudice – not to mention the advent of television with all the pressures that this mass exposure has brought to the game, and the sometimes cruel defensive play practised with crash tackling and claustrophobic marking, the international and World Cup referee has become the man very much in the middle – lonely, isolated, his every decision instantly replayed and analysed before an audience of a billion. His wish to be regarded as the 23rd player is rarely granted.

Consequently, top referees are a tough breed, or must be seen to be before, during and after the match, however much they may smart and hurt in private. They are expected by their judges to combine the wisdom of Solomon with the stamina of a long distance runner. Without doubt, it takes a very special man to submit himself willingly to derision, scorn, anger and often personal violence, and yet still be capable of making continually fair and impartial

Above: Stop-motion sequence of Geoff Hurst scoring the crucial third goal for England in the 1966 final. To this day, argument rages as to whether this goal should have been allowed. No positive evidence exists to show the ball actually crossing the goal line.
Right: England claim the goal as West Germany protest.

decisions, like the swift decision Gottfried Dienst was expected to make, and indeed made.

The Man Who Invented Refereeing

Sir Stanley Rous, CBE, spent 27 years as Secretary of the Football Association and 13 years as President of FIFA. This much loved and highly respected man has served football with great enthusiasm and dedication, shaping the international game and the World Cup as we now know it. At the same time he has been responsible for developing refereeing to cope with the new demands made upon referees in the world arena. This imposing yet gentle man is synonymous with the World Cup and when defeated by the narrowest of margins in the 1974 FIFA election in Frankfurt by Dr Joao Havelange, he was immediately made Honorary President of FIFA. Havelange has great respect for the man and his achievements and is the first to request his presence when the media's eyes are on

FIFA. Sir Stanley himself, even today, does all he can to help and advise the new President, never interfering or intruding, simply helping when asked to assist in an ever improving and growing FIFA.

Top referees are a tough breed, or must be seen to be before, during and after the match, however much they may smart and hurt in private

He was born in the village of Mutford, near Beccles in Suffolk in the spring of 1895. There was no sporting activity at all in the little village until the young Rous started his schooling. From the age of thirteen he attended the St John Leman School in Beccles, cycling every day back and forth to Mutford. On arriving at the school he knew nothing of football, but was quickly attracted to the game and soon became a member of the school team. After about a year he had the confidence to bring back a football to Mutford, with the sole intention of starting a football team there. The sporting educationalist and administrator was already present in this 14-year-old boy. He built up a team of local farmers, fishermen and their sons, taught them the rudiments of the game and created enough interest to arrange matches, conducted properly, within the village. Interest was soon created over the whole district, and other villages rapidly took up the game and organized their own teams.

In due course he was invited to play in goal for Kirkley Football Club, a member of the Norfolk and Suffolk Senior League. He was eventually asked to join Lowestoft FC but this was literally within days of joining his battalion, for the 1914–18 War was now to interrupt his education and footballing prowess. For the duration of the war , he served with the Royal Artillery in France, Egypt and Palestine. He played football for his battalion during those years and did a little refereeing in Egypt. When the war was over, he resumed his education at St Luke's, Exeter, where he was appointed captain of the football and the tennis teams. But his sporting days had been damaged by the war; he had suffered a shrapnel wound in Palestine which permanently affected his right wrist. So his refereeing experience in Egypt was soon put to use, and after a short while he was enjoying the task of refereeing.

He moved on to a schoolmaster's job at Watford Grammar School, where he taught and was sportsmaster from 1921 to 1934. It was very difficult to arrange football fixtures in those years, so rugby was played and Rous had the valuable experience of organising rugby matches and refereeing. During this time he progressed as a football referee and he was soon a qualified class I football referee. His progress was rapid and he was appointed linesman

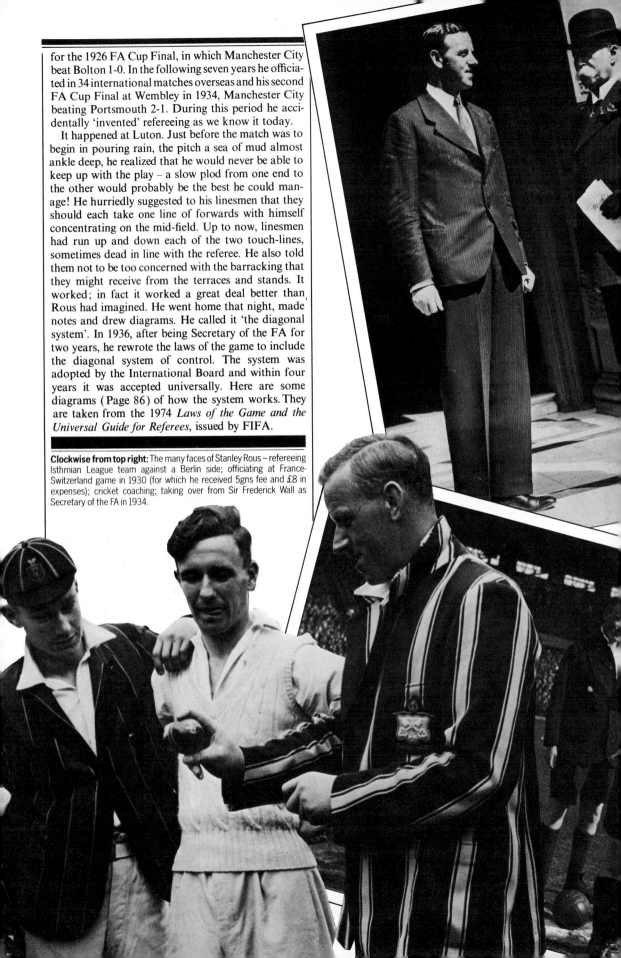

for the 1926 FA Cup Final, in which Manchester City beat Bolton 1-0. In the following seven years he officiated in 34 international matches overseas and his second FA Cup Final at Wembley in 1934, Manchester City beating Portsmouth 2-1. During this period he accidentally 'invented' refereeing as we know it today.

It happened at Luton. Just before the match was to begin in pouring rain, the pitch a sea of mud almost ankle deep, he realized that he would never be able to keep up with the play – a slow plod from one end to the other would probably be the best he could manage! He hurriedly suggested to his linesmen that they should each take one line of forwards with himself concentrating on the mid-field. Up to now, linesmen had run up and down each of the two touch-lines, sometimes dead in line with the referee. He also told them not to be too concerned with the barracking that they might receive from the terraces and stands. It worked; in fact it worked a great deal better than Rous had imagined. He went home that night, made notes and drew diagrams. He called it 'the diagonal system'. In 1936, after being Secretary of the FA for two years, he rewrote the laws of the game to include the diagonal system of control. The system was adopted by the International Board and within four years it was accepted universally. Here are some diagrams (Page 86) of how the system works. They are taken from the 1974 *Laws of the Game and the Universal Guide for Referees*, issued by FIFA.

Clockwise from top right: The many faces of Stanley Rous – refereeing Isthmian League team against a Berlin side; officiating at France-Switzerland game in 1930 (for which he received 5gns fee and £8 in expenses); cricket coaching; taking over from Sir Frederick Wall as Secretary of the FA in 1934.

THE DIAGONAL SYSTEM OF CONTROL

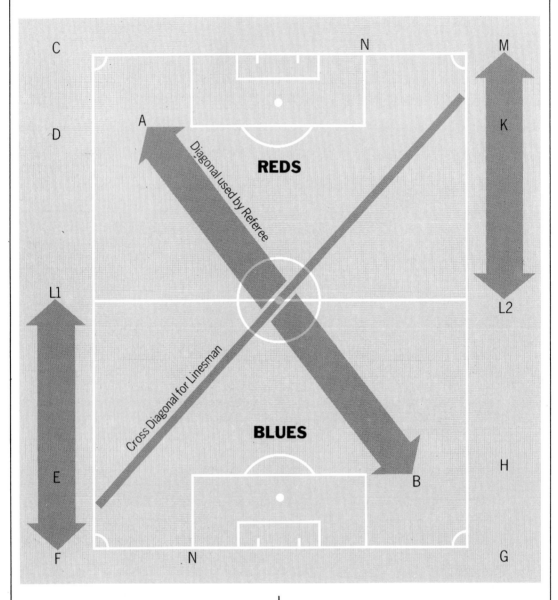

Diagram 1

The imaginary diagonal used by the Referee is the line A–B.

The opposite diagonal used by the Linesmen is adjusted to the position of the Referee; if the Referee is near A, Linesman L2 will be at a point between M and K. When the Referee is at B, Linesman L1 will be between E and F; this gives two officials control of the respective "danger zones", one at each side of the field.

Linesman L1 adopts the *Reds* as his side; Linesman L2 adopts the *Blues;* as *Red* forwards move towards Blue goal, Linesman L1 keeps in line with second last *Blue* defender so in actual practice he will rarely get into Red's half of the field. Similarly Linesman L2 keeps in line with

second last *Red* defender, and will rarely get into Blue's half.

At corner-kicks or penalty-kicks the Linesman in that half where the corner-kick or penalty-kick occurs positions himself at N and the Referee takes position (see Diagram 4 – corner-kick; Diagram 9 – penalty-kick).

The diagonal system fails if Linesman L2 gets between G and H when Referee is at B, or when Linesman L1 is near C or D when the Referee is at A, because there are *two* officials at the same place. This should be avoided.

(N.B. – Some Referees prefer to use the opposite diagonal, viz., from F to M, in which case the Linesmen should adjust their work accordingly.)

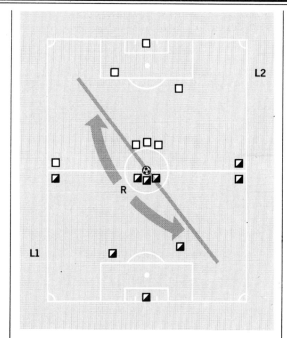

Diagram 2

Start of the game

Position of Referee at Kick-off – R.

Position of Linesmen – L1 and L2: in position with second last defender.

Players – □ and ◨

Diagonal followed by Referee A–B. Referee moves to diagonal along line ◁———▷ according to direction of attack.

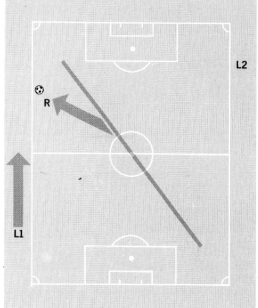

Diagram 3. (following on from diagram 2).

Development of the attack

Ball moves out to left wing, Referee (R) slightly off diagonal to be near play.

Linesman (L2) level with second last defender.

Two officials, therefore, up with play.

Linesman (L1) in position for clearance and possible counter-attack.

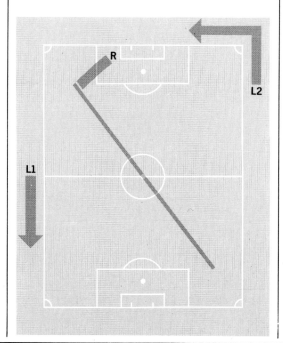

Diagram 4

The corner kick

Positions of officials the same no matter at which corner-area the kick is taken.

Referee (R) along line shown.

Linesman (L2) – in accordance with the instructions from the Referee the Linesman (L2) shall be near the corner flag or on the goal-line near the corner flag, to observe whether the ball is properly played, whether the opposing players are at proper distance (10 yards) ,whether the ball is behind the goal-line, or whether incidents have happened possibly hidden from the Referee.

Linesman (L1) in position for clearance and possible counter-attack.

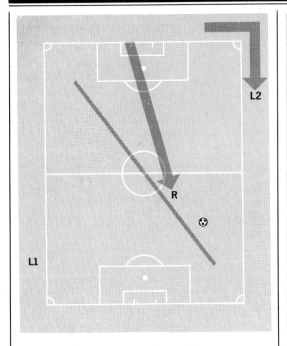

Diagram 5. (following on from diagram 4).

The counter-attack

Referee (R) sprints to regain correct position on diagonal path ——▷

(Note: The Referee who is physically fit is able to do this easily.)

Linesman (L2) hurries back to his correct position on the touch-line.

Linesman (L1) level with attack and in position to see infringements and indicate decisions until Referee regains his position.

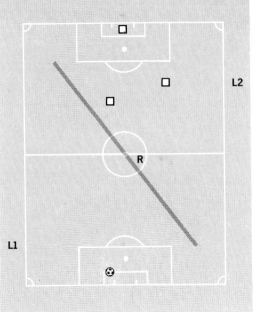

Diagram 6

The goal-kick

Referee (R) in midfield adjacent to central point of diagonal.

Linesman (L1) exercising watch over goal-kick, positioned in line with the penalty-area.

Linesman (L2) in position in line with second last defender pending a possible attack by side taking goal-kick.

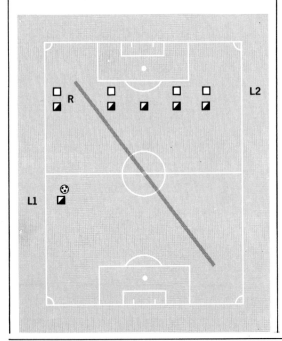

Diagram 7

The free-kick in mid-field

Players line up for kick □ and ◪. Referee (R) and Linesman (L2) in respective diagonal positions, level with players and able to judge accurately any questions of off-side or foul play. Linesman (L1) sees that kick is taken from correct position and also is in position for possible counter-attack.

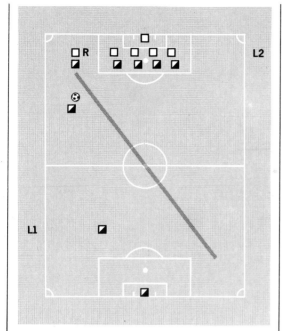

Diagram 8. (just outside penalty-area).

The free-kick near the goal

Players ☐ and ◪ line up for free-kick.

Referee (R) takes up his position just off his diagonal so that he is placed accurately to judge off-side. Linesman (L2) is more advanced but can watch for off-side and fouls and also is in a good position to act as goal judge in the event of a direct shot being taken.

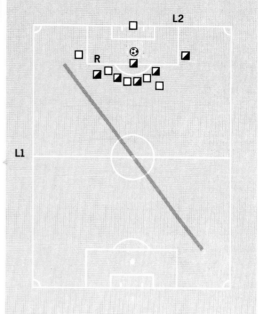

Diagram 9

The penalty-kick

Players ☐ and ◪ with the exception of the goalkeeper and kicker are shown outside the penalty-area and at least 10 yards from the ball – goalkeeper on goal-line.

Referee (R) is in position to see that kick is properly taken and that no encroachment takes place.

Linesman (L2) watches goalkeeper to see that he does not advance illegally and also acts as goal judge.

Linesman (L1) is in position should the goalkeeper save a goal and start a counter-attack.

Diagram 10

The throw-in

Ball out of play and Linesman (L2) is in position with second last defender indicating position of throw and to which side.

Referee (R) crosses from diagonal to centre of field, in the same manner as a defence covering a throw-in.

Linesman (L1) in position in line with his second last defender for the possible counter-attack.

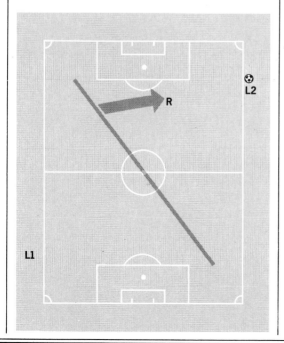

It was during his refereeing years that Stanley Rous became increasingly respected by both the English administrators of the game and FIFA, not just as a referee, where his theories could be proved in practice, but concerning the game generally where his comments were always lucid and of value.

He came to FIFA's notice when refereeing a match between Holland and Belgium in Amsterdam. The Executive Committee of FIFA happened to be meeting at the same time and in the same place. The FIFA officials thought he handled the match 'impeccably' and 'refereed in a large and sensible manner'. There was crowd trouble and instead of stopping play whilst calm was restored, which might have added to the stress of the situation, he carried on and order was swiftly achieved. He was appointed a Senior International Referee for this 'strict application of the rules and letting the game flow'.

Rous, like virtually all top-class referees and players, usually felt a little nervous before an international, but had no fear which might disturb his handling of the game. He always expected to be in charge, he had authority and through experience used it sensibly. There was one occasion, though, when he was touched with fear. It was a game between Hungary and Italy in Budapest – the first to have a live radio commentary – a stormy, gruelling match in which a Hungarian player's leg was broken. Rous managed to keep order until five minutes from time, when a savage tackle laid out another Hungarian. The crowd went wild – even the trainer didn't dare tread the pitch. Eighty thousand cardboard megaphones drowned the stadium in a screeching protest. The game was restarted with only two minutes remaining. Finding himself opposite the players' exit, Rous quickly blew for full-time. Afterwards, when listening to protests that he had ended the match early, he attempted no excuses. His answer was simple: 'I was the time-keeper'.

Players in general had great respect for Rous and his reputation. A French player learned how not to treat a top referee during a match that needed strict handling: he suddenly rushed up to Rous and said what he thought of him in pidgin English. Rous replied in pidgin English: 'You do not think much of my refereeing?' 'Bloody well no.' A slight pause, then: 'You had better get off then, you go, because I am staying on the pitch'. The player walked off the pitch very quietly.

As Secretary of the FA two of Rous's chief aims were developing the 'grass roots' of football – youth teams, youth competitions, schoolboy football – and the raising of refereeing standards and increasing the quantity of quality men. When he was elected President of FIFA at their Congress in 1961, two of his continuing priorities were developing the International Youth Tournament and holding the first International Referee's Course. He achieved this and progress was swiftly made.

In refereeing, England was once more teaching the world, for there is no doubt that England and Scotland had the best and most efficient referees when Rous arrived at FIFA Headquarters. Series of courses and seminars, first across Europe but then elsewhere,

Below: Rous with youthful players in Poland in 1971. Such visits as this over many years have done a great deal to encourage the grass roots of football and have been partly responsible for Sir Stanley being known across the world as 'Mr. Football', a richly deserved accolade for a man whose whole life has been devoted to the game.

Facing page: International referees are expected to deal with all manner of incidents on the pitch, often in the face of vociferous opposition from crowds and players alike.

'No person should be deprived of improving his sporting pursuits through lack of coaching and then personal application'

and continuing each year, have brought a uniform standard of refereeing throughout the world. Every member country of FIFA submits through their national association, each season, up to seven International Referees, and they are expected to be of a high standard.

'There is no substitute for skill' is a quote used hundreds of times by Sir Stanley. He preached this

Each official is carefully selected by FIFA from lists submitted by member countries around the world. They are subjected to rigorous training, both physical and mental, are taught how to cope with language barriers in international matches, and in turn advise FIFA's Referee's Committee on improving control.
Facing page: FIFA referee and his linesman take the field.
Centre right: Angel Norberto Coerezza of Argentina.
Centre left: Pat Partridge listens patiently to what Cruyff has to say.
Below: Ken Burns lays it on the line for QPR's Don Masson.

belief right across the sporting world to players and referees of all sports; 'no person should be deprived of improving his sporting pursuits through lack of coaching and then personal application.'

Through his years with FIFA, travelling the world and setting up referee's coaching courses, having films made on the subject and constantly bringing out publications, Rous has without doubt brought about an immense uniformity in applying the laws in theory and, most important, in practice on the pitch. Here is an extract from the foreword by Sir Stanley to FIFA's *Handbook for Referee Instructors* (1976) which sums up the attitude he has held for years:

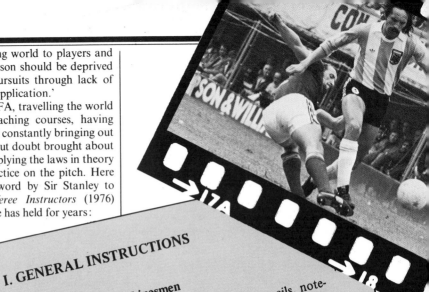

I. GENERAL INSTRUCTIONS

1. To Referees and Linesmen

The basic and general equipment of Referees — watches, whistles, pencils, note-pads, etc. — are universally known and need no repetition here, but the great extension of international football at all levels has brought some further problems and points for referees to note.

In all such cases, Referees should be assured that their home association will offer them all possible help and advice, and they should never hesitate to ask.

One of the most important factors in modern international football is climate and, to some extent, changes of altitude. European Referees, for example, are now employed quite extensively in South America and Africa and even further afield, and they should always satisfy themselves as to the climate they must expect, with its obvious influence on clothing and, for that matter, the diet they should follow when in the foreign country.

In this matter of clothing, one point cannot be too strongly stressed — Referees must establish in advance the colours of the competing teams. The dark blue or black jackets and shorts which referees wear do not normally clash, but referees must make quite certain of this in advance. Again, the home association will help in this matter.

Linesmen should carry their flags unfurled.

Referees must be quite clear as to their responsibilities under the F.I.F.A. Regulations for match reports, which include submitting their reports to the Secretary of F.I.F.A. promptly.

The Referee must not allow trainers or any other persons to enter the field of play while the game is in progress unless they receive a signal from him to do so; he must also prevent coaching by trainers and club officials from the boundary lines.

If a Referee should fail to report misconduct, which comes under his notice, and it is proved to the satisfaction of the National Association or affiliated Association that such misconduct was of a nature that required investigation, he shall be suspended or otherwise dealt with.

2. To National Associations

National Associations may submit each season the names of seven (maximum) International Referees.

The National Associations are responsible for placing the names of International Referees on the list, and the Referees for International matches shall be selected by the two National Associations concerned.

In an International match Linesmen may be senior (National) Referees, other than those on the above mentioned list.

Before definitely agreeing on the choice of a Referee and Linesmen of a new country, National Associations concerned shall ask a neutral country to su them with the names of the three best Referees at that time. The name of the Referee selected to control the match must appear on the list of International Referees of F.I.F.A.

For floodlight matches Linesmen should be provided with fluorescent flags.

It is misconduct for any Association or Club or any player, official or member of any Association or Club, to offer or attempt to offer, either directly or indirectly, any consideration whatever to another Club, player or players of any Club, with a view to influencing the result of a match. It is misconduct for any Club, player or players to accept any such consideration. In any case where this concerns the Referee, the competent Football Authority shall expel him from football, and if the bribery related to a match at which the referee officiated then it shall be replayed.

If the competent Authority of a National Association is informed that unsporting incidents have taken place unnoticed by the Referee who was thus unable to report thereon, an inquiry should be instituted and the evidence of neutral persons be obtained.

3. For International Matches

In accordance with F.I.F.A. Regulations, referees appointed to International Matches and those acting as linesmen are entitled to the refund of travelling expenses (railway travel and sleeping accommodation 1st class; by boat 1st class and by plane tourist class or 1st class, depending on the duration of the journey).

The Referee and Linesmen are entitled to a daily allowance of 120.— Swiss Francs in respect of the expenses incurred on their journey (food, insurance and other expenses). This amount and travel expenses must be paid to the Referee and Linesmen, for the necessary number of days away from home including the days of travel, on the day of the match by the Association organizing the match.

The hotel expenses and board are at the charge of the Association organizing the match.

The home Association should arrange for the Referee and Linesmen to be paid in a currency which is negotiable in their own country.

The Referee and Linesmen should assure themselves that their passport is in order and that they have a visa if it is required.

Before the Referee and Linesmen arrive at the city or town in which the match is to be played, they should notify the Association of the time of their arrival, and whether by aeroplane or train, and the home Association should arrange for them to be met at the airport or railway station. The Association should also arrange for interpreter to be available to them during the whole of their stay.

The above regulations apply to inter-club matches except that the amounts paid ... differ according to the rules of the competition under which the match is ...

'The work FIFA has done so far should have created a nucleus of people in most countries able to undertake the leadership of courses. Where this has not yet happened then, of course, FIFA will continue to help . . . . Refereeing has become more difficult in recent years for two reasons: firstly, there is a much greater number of games played at a higher level, international club matches are increasing, and they require good officials who are not only familiar with the laws but courageous in interpreting them. The types of player are changing also, and there is need for greater insight into how to handle players and how to deal with situations on the field involving this new breed of player, especially when the stakes are now so high. Increasingly the game needs men of good intellect to act as officials, men who not only understand the grammar of the laws but the spirit of the game.'

CHAPTER 2

Planning of Courses

The planning of a course must take into consideration many local factors and variations. Adjustments to meet local conditions and requirements are inevitable, but the most important factor is the time available.

The most likely lengths of course are:

1. One-day course
2. A week-end course
3. A five-day course

There may be longer courses, but these will be far less frequent because of the difficulties of organisation and the limited number of students who could find the time to participate. The one-day course would have to be selective in topics and intention and material should be drawn from the week-end course syllabus.

1. Week-end course

Probably the most convenient length of time for a week-end course would take in the Friday evening, use all of Saturday to end Sunday afternoon.

Friday evening:
Reception
Official opening of Course – outlining the purpose of the Course.
Films

Saturday morning:
Lecture — General Topic
Group work — Laws 2-6
Break
Lecture — General Topic
Group work — Laws 7-10
Lunch

Saturday afternoon:
Lecture — Laws 11 and 12 —
supported by films
Group work — discussion
Tea
Lecture — General Topic
Dinner

Saturday evening:
Films
Recreational

Sunday morning:
Lecture — Laws 13 and 14
Group work — Laws 15, 16 and 17
Break
Lecture — The Use and Abuse of 'Advantage'
Lunch

Sunday afternoon:
Discussion on points raised in lectures.
Answers to special questions on the Laws of the Game (submitted in writing previously)
Summing up and closure

The likely topics for the general lectures indicated above can be selected from the much fuller list which follows in respect of the five-day residential course. The particular selection, in view of the more limited time, would have to pay attention to the needs of the students and the particular objects of the course.

2. Five-day course

The five-day course, will allow of a much fuller treatment of various topics. It would also enable more work to be done which is important to the course, but extraneous to its immediate programme, such as visits to matches and organisation of physical training and tests; in the extended course there would also be more opportunity for practical demonstrations and far more practical work of all sorts.

CO-OPERATION
BETWEEN REFEREE AND LINESMEN

Co-operation between Referee and Linesmen – Law VI

In the Laws of the game set out in the foregoing pages there are no instructions as to the relative positioning of Referee and Linesmen during a game. There are, however, instructions in Laws V and VI with regard to powers and duties of Referee and Linesmen which rightly interpreted would mean co-operation. Law VI stipulates that two Linesmen shall be appointed, whose duty (subject to the decision of the Referee) shall be:

(a) To indicate *when* the ball is out of play.

(b) To indicate when the ball has crossed the goal-line and whether a corner-kick or a goal-kick is to be awarded.

(c) To indicate which side is entitled to the throw in.

(d) To assist the Referee in carrying out the game in accordance with the Laws.

The assistance referred to in (d) is:

(1) Signalling when the *whole* of the ball is out of play.

(2) Indicating *which* side is entitled to the corner-kick, the goal-kick, or the throw-in.

(3) Calling the attention of the Referee to rough play or ungentlemanly conduct.

(4) Giving an opinion on any point on which the Referee may consult him.

Neutral Linesmen

The assistance referred to above is best given by *Neutral Linesmen*. A limitation is placed upon *Club Linesmen* because points (2), (3) and (4) are not usually referred to Linesmen who are not neutral. In case of Neutral Linesmen they must be used as *Assistant Referees*. It is appreciated that there must be a different attitude adopted by the Referee in this case, because in effect there are *three* officials supervising the play; the *Referee* remains as principal official, but the Linesmen are there to assist him to control the game in a proper manner.

Club Linesmen

To get the most effective co-operation from *Club Linesmen* the following procedure should be adopted:

(1) *Both* Club Linesmen should report to the Referee *before* the start of the match, and receive his instructions, and be informed that no matter what may be their personal opinion the decision of the Referee is final, and must not be questioned.

(2) The work allotted to them as *Club* Linesmen is to signal *when* the ball is *entirely* over the touch-line, and to indicate *which* side is entitled to the throw-in, subject always to the decision of the Referee.

It Wouldn't Happen in the Park!

Dawn broke on the day of the Munich World Cup Final in 1974. Jack Taylor, the designated referee, was sleeping soundly in his hotel room. The Englishman was in a deep sleep, regaining his strength after the initial excitement and complications that go with being appointed to officiate the most important international match for four years. This man, butcher by trade and a widely recognised world-class referee, would wake in his own time and then calmly prepare himself for the match of his life – the ultimate achievement for any referee.

By the time he had checked his equipment, selected his whistle and placed it with care into its case, left the hotel and arrived at the stadium, some tension had naturally built up inside him. But after checking the selected match ball, talking to and briefing his linesmen (there would be no communication problem here), checking team lists, and examining boot studs, he was feeling more tense and tummy nerves were felt. The toss-up was with a commemorative 'Wild Life Fund' coin, a rather special idea instigated by the Fund's international patron at the time, Prince Bernhard of the Netherlands. It was seconds before the kick off and the organization had been perfect. Suddenly from the corner of his eye Taylor noticed a man running towards the touch-line and then a certain amount of commotion. The running man turned out to be Ken Aston, Chairman of FIFA's Technical Committee and responsible for the tournament's referees. Like a picture suddenly coming into focus the whole pitch was taken in and Taylor could see clearly that the four corner flags were missing! On such an occasion, when organisation had been so perfect, when every aspect had been checked and double-checked, how could this possibly happen? Corner flags would never be forgotten in preparing a junior team match in the park on a Sunday morning! From up in the stands, Ken Aston's eagle eye had pinpointed, almost unconsciously, this amazing blunder. One man then proceeded to travel to each corner of the pitch and insert the missing flags; it was a comical sight in the circumstances. Taylor found he could now relax; smiling outwardly and laughing inside, he blew the whistle and the 1974 World Cup Final was under way.

A Brave Referee

The match started in an extraordinary way. The crowd was hushed and Taylor claims today that he knew almost immediately that something was going to happen in those early seconds which would require a rapid and definite decision. From the kick-off the Dutch strung together an attack of 17 passes; the crowd was delighted to see such sweet footballing expertise and amazed that there was not a single German tackle until the ball was a yard inside the penalty box. This was the incident that Taylor's instinct told him to expect, so he had made sure that he was three or four yards behind the players concerned. Cruyff was floored in the box, Taylor blew and pointed to the penalty spot. The stadium erupted; within one minute of the final commencing Taylor had handed the Dutch a penalty. The decision was correct and at the moment it happened Taylor

Facing page: Argentinian manager and coach escort Albrecht from the field after dismissal in the 1966 West Germany game.
Below: Jack Taylor and his linesmen take the field.

was able to be one hundred per cent certain. Television and radio commentators were telling the world what a brave referee this was, how right he was, asking their audience to imagine themselves giving such a decision in Munich with the West German crowd breathing down his neck.

But Taylor is the first to say bravery didn't come into it; that was the last thing on his mind. To him this match, once it was under way, became the orange shirts against the white, and he had awarded a penalty against the whites, for according to the laws of the game, they had committed an offence which demanded such retribution. Equally, should he have failed to carry out this honest decision it would not have been through cowardice, he would simply have failed in giving an immediate and decisive response to the offence. He would then have let down not just FIFA but everything the international game and the World Cup represents.

For a while now the match was exacting to officiate, and Taylor was soon aware of the Germans' planned tight marking of the Dutch, especially Vogts' shadowing of Cruyff. This was a key pairing to watch and very soon Taylor was convinced that should Cruyff have to leave the pitch for any reason, Vogts would have followed him!

Taylor then awarded the Germans a return penalty. Television and film have shown his decision to be correct, though at the time this totally professional man was not totally convinced that he *was* right. Again instinct told him it was indeed an offence by the Dutch, to be punished with the 'spot-kick', but the angle from which he saw the offence was not ideal. However, he was executing the laws of the game in the correct manner, for the German player was within the Dutch penalty area and although the ball was two to three feet ahead of him, there was, or seemed to be, a definite tripping offence committed against him – attempting to trip would have sufficed.

After this incident the Dutch became very tetchy and Taylor was fully stretched to help the game flow and be as memorable as it turned out to be. The man deserved to be regarded as a twenty-third player performing at the height of his ability, but because he had to award two penalties out of three goals, the media gave him as much coverage as any of the outstanding players. Once again, though for the best of reasons, he was isolated as the 'man in the middle'.

Perhaps it is only the average referee – as long as the game makes no special demands – who can truly be absorbed and survive with little notice? But then the average referee would not be chosen to scale such refereeing heights, and World Cup matches do tend to make special demands!

Great Developments in Four Years

It has to be admitted that the overall standard of refereeing in the 1966 World Cup left a lot to be desired. The FIFA Referees' Committee for this hard and defensive tournament did not plan sufficiently

Right: Jack Taylor in action around the world and **(far right)** after investiture with the OBE.

well to encourage a good standard of refereeing. In hindsight they know they should have done, because the international scene since the 1962 Finals had been showing a demand for firm and uniform application of the laws. Sir Stanley Rous was aware of this and consequently so was FIFA, but time hadn't developed the standards required; poor organisation for the arriving top 30 referees in England didn't help. Training facilities were supplied for them at Queens Park Rangers' ground, but they only trained if they wished to and overall they were left to their own devices. There was a shortage of interpreters to help any kind of overall understanding and this badly affected what few talks were held before the finals began. The men arrived just before the first matches so that there was little chance, with or without a language barrier, of any feeling of comradeship developing. The large group of British referees didn't help much, as they tended to keep themselves very much apart. Probably they didn't realise it at the time, nor were they aware of looking at the game solely through English eyes. Sadly, they didn't or couldn't pay enough attention to the points of view of the foreign officiators, who were forced to remain apart. Consequently communication between referees and linesmen during matches suffered badly (the final itself was an example). It was the tournament of controversial bookings and sending-offs: the Rattin incident described earlier, English referee Jim Finney – much admired internationally – sending off two Uruguayans, Troche the captain and Silva in the match against West Germany. Finney had a police escort from the pitch.

Brazil left the tournament feeling that teams had been allowed to kick them out of World Cup glory, Uruguay and Argentina packed their bags and left showing considerable bitterness. By coincidence in their trouble-strewn matches it was a German and an English referee that had officiated at their dismissals. In reality, blame could not be laid at the confused referees' feet; it was lack of overall foresight, for not

Above: Ken Aston stands firm during near-riot scenes in the 1962 Italy-Chile World Cup game as Ferrini of Italy is ordered off.
Centre: 'Look at that!' as Argentina's Villa accelerates.
Below: Clive Thomas of Wales.
Facing page: 'What a stinker!' Gordon Hill gives his considered opinion.

102

enough thought had been given to the complications which could and indeed did arise.

FIFA worked extremely hard in the intervening years to make sure Mexico would not suffer in the same way in the organisation of referees, even if styles of play continued to be dominated by hard defensive tactics. There was also the worry of altitude and rarefied air to be taken into account by players and referees alike.

The FIFA Referees' Committee

Below is an extract from Article 26 of the *Statutes of FIFA*.

1. The Referees' Committee shall consist of a Chairman and eight Members nominated by the Executive Committee.
2. Its duties shall be:

    (a) to prepare the official translations of the Laws of the Game and of any alterations made thereto;

    (b) to give decisions regarding the application of the Laws of the Game;

    (c) to propose to the Executive Committee the alterations to the Laws of the Games to be submitted to the International Football Association Board;

    (d) to compile a list of Referees qualified to control International Matches from the nominations submitted by the National Associations;

    (e) to establish as far as possible uniformity in methods of refereeing and application of the Laws;

    (f) to be responsible for the editing of the section 'Laws of the Game' in the official Bulletin of FIFA;

    (g) to organize Courses for International Referees and for those responsible for the education and the preparation of Referees in their countries, directly or conjointly with other organizations;

    (h) to form a group of lecturers who, from time to time, and according to the necessities, take part in Courses and Reunions organized by the Referees' Committee;

    (i) to prepare and publish memoranda, books, booklets, films and other visual aids;

    (k) to collect a library of such aids (i) in FIFA House for use at Courses and to lend them to National Associations;

    (l) to appoint the Referees to Competitions organized by FIFA according to the demand of the various National Associations;

    (m) to ensure that each national association has a properly constituted Referees' Committee, and to ascertain that these committees function satisfactorily.

    (n) The duties specified in para. 2 (g), (i) and (k) above and the resulting financial responsibilities shall be reported to the Finance Committee.

Sir Stanley Rous had Ken Aston appointed as Deputy Chairman of the Referees' Committee in 1968, and he was to be responsible for the organising and selection (with the Committee) of the thirty referees for the coming tournament. This ex-player who, through injury, took up refereeing at the age of 20 – he qualified in 1936 – took charge of the 1963 FA Cup Final (Manchester United versus Leicester City), the 1961 Inter-Continental Final (Real Madrid versus Peñarol) and the opening match in the 1962 World Cup. Aston has a very amusing memory of this occasion, although it was less than amusing at the time. Naturally there had been great excitement for the opening ceremony and Aston had arrived at the stadium at one for the kick-off at three. At 2.20 he was still waiting for the selected match ball, with correct weight and pressure and countersigned by the Referees' Committee. He had the ball sent for. At 2.40 no ball had arrived and at 2.55 he led the teams out into the packed stadium with a sinking feeling – he wasn't carrying the match ball! During the next five minutes he called in a number of the 'kick-in' balls from surprised players and desperately searched for a 'possible' amongst the tatty leather puddings! He decided on one sad object and the game got under way. Meanwhile a FIFA representative was sent post-haste to purchase a ball for the opening match of this World Cup, and in the later stages of the game a spanking new ball was finally bounced onto the pitch!

The President had made a wise choice in selecting Aston for the difficult task that lay ahead. He had very firm ideas of how to achieve the required results that the footballing nations and the media felt could not be accomplished. Aston's views were in the main complementary to the President's, so he was given much support and encouragement and made Chairman. Aston announced that the concern for a high quality of refereeing during the tournament in the heat and suspect atmosphere of Mexico would minimise the difficulties experienced in 1966. A bold statement like that from the man encouraged him to remark 'I'm not like the man who was once conceited – I'm now perfect!' and in fact it was this appointment that resulted in refereeing 'coming of age' on international pitches. On reflection Aston likes to feel that in Mexico the foundations of a good house were built, Germany added the decorations, and that Argentina will add the furnishings!

Aston had decided that for the Mexican World Cup the referees would be welded into the seventeenth team, that the communication problem would be resolved once and for all, and that all 30 referees should work together closely. His desire was that every man should be as highly trained as a boxer, superbly fit and able to relax mentally whenever possible. He knew he would be dealing with men who regarded themselves as professionals in attitude, application and dedication – the honour and the

---

Facing page: Brazilian midfield player Everaldo lies on the ground after being flattened by an England player in the 1970 World Cup. The Israeli referee watches the famous Brazilian trainer Amerigo as he gives attention to ensure there is no time-wasting.

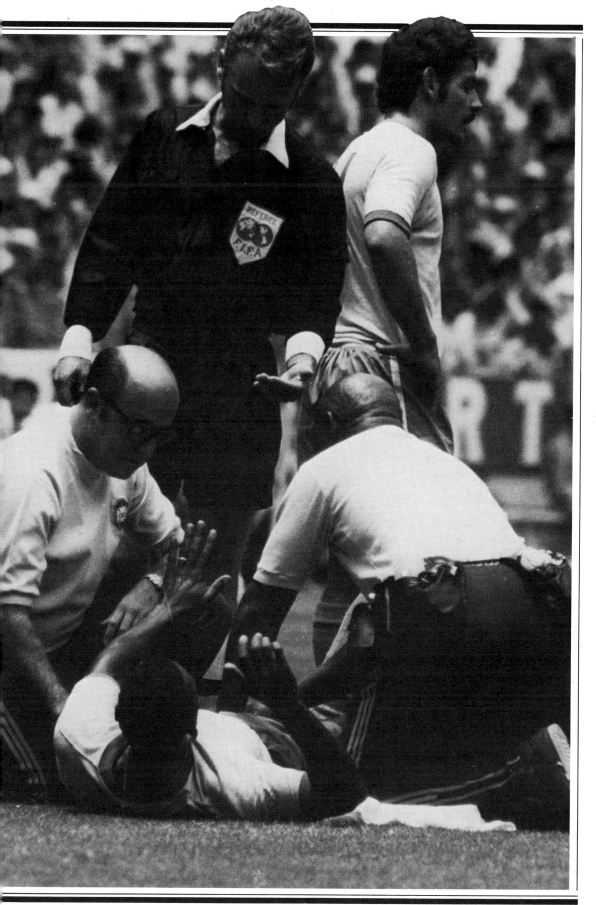

challenge being their just reward – for on World Cup level the selected *arbitres* have no official association and are not paid one franc for their match work.

Two weeks before the competition opened, all the referees arrived at FIFA's request in Mexico City. Apart from the programme set by Aston and his distinguished colleagues, it was felt that acclimatisation was also necessary. As it turned out, the feared high altitude caused very little problems – which surprised many eminent doctors who had warned of much danger to the competing players and concern for older referees, such as Aly Kandill from Egypt who was now fifty. As it was, oxygen was sometimes given to individuals in losing teams; winners usually managed brisk exits from the stadium and not a single referee called for the aid of the oxygen mask. Medical tests on the referees were carried out every day, to check on their reaction to the altitude.

For this tournament every referee was given training gear and track suits and for the first time ever in a World Cup, a top coach was appointed to make sure every member referee was physically at his peak. A West German, Dettmar Cramer, was given the task. No referee was allowed to miss any of the training sessions conducted in a first-class sports club which contained every facility that was required. Cramer put every man through his paces and concentrated on building him up, not reducing him to a gasping invalid. After training a kick-about game was held and great team spirit was quickly developed. After this lectures were held at a conference centre equipped with all the electronic trappings to avoid the language barrier, instant translation being available through headphones. After the lectures, groups would break up for seminars. The main languages used were French, English, German and Spanish, so the men joined groups according to their language, to discuss and argue points raised in the lectures.

An example of how well this welding together of 30 men was progressing and how comradeship quickly blossomed was the situation of Kandill of Egypt and Klein of Israel. Being in the same seminar group, men from two opposing and hostile countries were not likely to become bosom friends, and relationships were strained. Yet by the fourth day tension had dropped away and friendship through a common sporting interest developed.

FIFA, through these lectures, films and seminars, was asking the men to express their views and say what they wanted. The approaches and interpretations of South American refereeing was compared with European standards and through discussion uniformity was agreed on in the application of laws and co-operation between a referee and his linesmen. Additionally, a special silent film of World Cup incidents had been shown early on in this programme of preparation. The men had watched it and were asked to discuss in theory how they would cope, but in a real and practical way. A week later they saw the film again, this time with sound and the decisions overall were uniform with FIFA's narration.

FIFA then sent the film to each competing nation with a memorandum of all the points that the referees had agreed on and that FIFA had approved to every

national coach. The memorandum was also given to the press.

This was the tournament in which FIFA had agreed with the referees to use yellow and red cards, to let players know clearly that they were being cautioned or sent off and alleviate doubts and confusions because of language barriers. There would thus be no repeat of the ugly sending-off scenes in the 1966 tournament. This idea was borrowed from America, where it was invented to cope with their language difficulties caused by so many immigrant players.

Despite all this, by the time the first match kicked off in Mexico City, it was still felt by some that all the strict refereeing preparations would bear little fruit. It was the complete opposite. The Mexico versus Russia match was not an exciting affair, but Tschenscher kept it well in control and dealt out five yellow cards. In reality all the work and preparation was immediately shown to be working and the standard of refereeing was set. In this hot and temperamental land not a single player was sent off throughout the summer.

This Happy Breed

Within the game good referees are now shown a deal of respect. FIFA has taught the world how important a first-class officiator is to an international game and, of course, this attitude has spread to nations' domestic games, where the stakes for winning increase year in and year out. Referees are happier now, knowing that in general their skills will be recognised and backed

to the full. Their ability to manage men, to communicate and to show understanding, discipline and humour is recognised whatever their colour, creed and continent. On the World Cup scene every referee is assessed and given marks for his performances by two men appointed by the Executive Committee: one who looks at the game as a whole, the other specifically at the referee. And on the general international scene every referee has his assessors, and it is on the results he achieves through the assessor's experienced eyes that will help him climb or slip down the ladder of progress. However, referees now feel that there is no pressure put on them by officialdom; all they are asked is to satisfy their conscience, show courage and please themselves, and in that way in all probability they will please their assessors.

They know that they are being helped to progress in every area of this specialised field, for FIFA and all the international committees at all times examine and help these men in enormously demanding positions. The 1974 World Cup was a perfect example of how, once more, in the four years after the final whistle blew in Mexico, FIFA had looked carefully at what would be needed in Munich and what improvements could be made.

For example, 'running the line' – expert referees finding themselves chosen as linesmen for a match, and having very little experience in the job – was vastly improved. Liberties with goal-keepers taking more than the allowed 'four steps rule' were tightened. Dissent from a player was clamped down on. Team time-wasting was watched with extra care. A decision on treatment for an injured player on the pitch was revised, though this was to prove a difficult point. Referees would have to assess the extent of injury quickly, for it is common for a player to feign injury and make it look worse in the hope of gaining the advantage through a free kick, or allowing the team doctor to pass on tactics from the bench, or holding up play to help the team reorganise if under pressure, or maybe simply because he is temperamentally suited to being a good actor and just enjoys making extra drama out of the unwritten plot – the match! Now a referee clearly understood that if a prostrate player was not seriously hurt the flow of the game should not be interrupted and if the injury was of a slight nature, then the player could be treated, but must leave the field of play and not return until the referee allowed him back. Obviously a point like this would at times receive criticism, especially from excitable coaches and partisan crowds, but in the main the brief given to the referees over this subject was dealt uniformally in a good and sensible manner. Munich was another good refereeing tournament and there is every reason to believe that with FIFA's policies unchanged, Argentina in 1978 will be just as good. But with correct preparation and video-recorded showings of each match the morning after for appraisal and examination, this group of men, through thick and thin, will remain a happier breed.

Facing page: The first international referee's course organised by FIFA, held in Switzerland in 1938.
Above: FIFA referee's conference in Olympia, Greece.
Left: FIFA referee's committee relax in Madrid.

Towards Argentina

There have been and continue to be many excellent referees, some great characters, and some that crowds have found it hard to hate. Take Arthur Ellis of England, who was involved in the infamous 'Battle of Berne' and who, at one moment during the awful scenes, literally dragged two players over the touch-line to cool off! Or Armando Marques of Brazil, a professional referee, who may be temperamental but is still a great referee. It isn't the money that makes a professional referee, it's dedication – a theme Marques would agree on. This man is a showman and if you didn't know his name or the look of the man, you'd know who it was by his habit of never blowing his whistle at the kick-off – he just waves a finger. Jim Finney of England had a style of his own and great common sense in handling players. His 'style of simplicity' was much admired across the world. A modern disciplinarian is Clive Thomas of Wales, who lets nothing go and at times ploughs a lone furrow as far as footballing officialdom is concerned, but his results in the 1974 World Cup were top marks in two matches. He is a strong candidate for 1978, however stern an image he presents. There have been and hopefully will continue to be the refereeing 'diplomats', calm, collected and always striving to let the game flow. Their critics call out that these men just want a quiet life on the pitch, but their results speak for themselves and in the meantime they have gained much popularity. Leo Horn of the Netherlands and Istvan Zsolt of Hungary are examples of such referees. Bobby Davidson of Scotland and Rudi Glockner of East Germany are others recognised and recognisable for their achievements. Youssoupha N'Diaye of Senegal – the Black Pearl – tall and black as ebony, is a new and striking referee to reach the World Cup recognition. In 1974 he had one match in the tournament and was excellent. There is every possibility he will be chosen for Argentina, as long as he is available – it is not unknown in Black Africa for a referee to be imprisoned for a short while, for if a president of one state does not approve of a serious decision made by the official, it has been known for a word to be spoken in the ear of the president of the offending referee's state, resulting in police waiting for the arrival of the referee's homebound plane and a quick escort to the local prison!

Apart from N'Diaye and Thomas, who are the other possibles to be flown to the Argentine by FIFA? Ramon Barreto of Uruguay, a businessman from Montevideo, internationally very experienced, who refereed two matches in Munich; Arnaldo Cezar Coelho from Brazil, a teacher in Rio, who has made definite strides in the international scene; Tony Boskovic, born in Australia of Yugoslavian extraction, a salesman who showed up well in the one match he refereed in the Munich finals and has the advantage of speaking four languages fluently; the Argentinian, Angel Norberto Coerezza, hailing from Buenos Aries, a business administrator who has no World Cup final experience but plenty on the international front; the excellent Ferdinand Biwersi of West Germany, a linesman in Munich, who has

'He will see, decide and act, impartially and honestly, and like any good player he will admit to himself his mistakes and know whether his performance was good or bad'

developed well in international matches; Pat Partridge of England, born in Bishop Auckland, who owns a small dairy farm in Northumbria, who had no World Cup matches in Munich, but is widely popular on the international arena; Alberto Michelotti of Italy; Robert Wurtz, the Frenchman who officiated the European Cup Final in 1977; Dogan Babacan of Turkey, who had a single match in Munich and in the same year refereed the European Cup semi-final, Celtic versus Atletico Madrid. It was a card-happy experience for him, cautioning four Atletico players and two from Celtic and having to send off three Spaniards. He is a brave referee!

These are the men amongst a host of others who will be selected from FIFA's vast list of recommended and internationally experienced referees – it represents a pleasing problem for FIFA that the list will be wide, including good names put forward by many young and progressing football nations. FIFA can comply with their duty of producing the best, and their training work over the continents has, and will continue to produce a great number of talented 'men you love to hate'.

For watchers of the game arguments will always be endless on whether the man in the middle is totally neutral – for every moment of the match – from the lower regions of nations' domestic football leagues to the exalted finals of a World Cup. But for a first-class referee the match will always be the 'reds' versus the 'whites'. He will see, decide and act, impartially and honestly, and like any good player he will admit to himself his mistakes and know whether his performance was good or bad. A good international referee is a man of substance, educated and of a mature nature. Off the field he must impress officials, statesmen, politicians and the broad section of VIPs whom he will meet; he is a true footballing ambassador.

Top: Referee Piot tosses up, Holland-Belgium game 1977.
Centre: An incident in a Brazil-Poland World Cup game.
Below: Making the draw for the 1974 World Cup.

TAMPA BAY TO TIMBUKTU

Three developing football nations, three different cultures, three different approaches to a common aim: to develop domestic football to such an extent that they may become internationally successful, competing with the established giants of football across the world and eventually qualifying for the World Cup tournament. In the swamps of Florida, on the sands of Tunisia and below the shimmering mountains in Iran, they are learning to play the game of the century. Time, effort and money is being lavished on new national teams in the belief that one day football's most glittering prize – the World Cup trophy – will be theirs.

Each nation in its own individual and characteristic way is making great inroads towards achieving its aim. Unless Iran's style and technique suddenly disappears they will be in the Argentine in 1978. If Tunisia continue to battle away with their usual enthusiasm and talent they could be alongside Iran at the opening ceremony in Buenos Aries, and should the United States continue to progress so fast with

Facing page top left: Moore and Pele playing in the USA in 1976 – old adversaries united at last.
Facing page top right: Eusebio with the fruits of success with Las Vegas Quicksilvers.
Facing page below: George Best in full flight for Los Angeles Aztecs. After a chequered career he found relative stability in the USA.
Below: Young Mexican players in training for the semi-final of the FIFA/Coca-Cola Junior World Cup, 1977.

their multi-million dollar soccer gamble they will be contenders for the World Cup crown in the 1980s.

These are three colourful and determined 'new' footballing nations which deserve a closer look.

Iran

Iran, unless disaster strikes, will be one of the sixteen finalists to parade its national flag in the River Plate Stadium on 1 June 1978. This proud nation will surely show the world football audience, for the first time, how well it has learned its footballing skills and how quickly it has developed into a major footballing nation. Iran has the right to compete with the élite in the World Cup, because the country has applied itself in a disciplined and methodical manner, spending sensibly and employing only the best coaches and trainers. In every way football is an expression of the development of their modern society. The players are expected to devote themselves unsparingly and, in return, to expect financial reward. The philosophy is simple – give all, receive all. Players do strive to give everything they can and it is an attitude that should be observed and taken note of by many footballers across the world, who take all they can without giving much in return.

Everyone who has an interest in football should be amazed that the Iranian game has made such rapid strides, since a national league was only formed some five years ago. Indeed, the league was only a year old

when Iran just failed to reach the 1974 World Cup; They lost narrowly on aggregate in the Asian zone final to Australia, winning 2-0 at home, losing 3-0 away. In 1977 the same two nations battled it out again for the right to fly to the Argentine. After already having drawn with South Korea away and beating Hong Kong at home, the 1-0 victory over Australia in Melbourne gave the team sweet revenge and an immedate tang of Argentine air.

This country – ringed with shimmering mountain ranges and flooded by sunlight – is a high plateau bounded in the north by the Caspian Sea and in the south by the Persian Gulf and the Sea of Oman. This is the land of one of the world's earliest known civilizations. The Aryans gave the country its name 'Iran' or 'Land of the Aryans'. The powerful Aryan tribes and the Persians united under Cyrus the Great and gave the world two of the most important concepts in history – one god and a political empire. From the seventh century AD Iran became a centre of Islamic civilization, producing a host of philosophers, mathematicians, astronomers, physicians and poets – Omar Khayam is a name that immediately springs to mind.

The hunter will know of the unspoiled areas in which he can track down a variety of game, and wrestling enthusiasts will know that their sport is traditionally Iran's national pastime – the country has produced many international champions. Gymnastics and water polo are now two fast-growing leisure sports, but the biggest sporting interest is in the rapid development of football, a sport that is precocious in its progress here. Should the world audience see Iran as a competing nation in the World Cup finals, then football will be instantly recognised as the national sport.

Tehran is the capital city and houses a superbly equipped stadium, where in 1974 the seventh Asian Games were successfully held. Since then the emphasis has been on football, with confidence in steady progress only wavering slightly when the 1974 World Cup finals eluded them by a goal average of one. Obviously Iran has the financial resources to aid its footballing programme, and the Shah himself has enthusiastically supported the aims and ideals of his football association.

But in football you cannot buy success without the intelligence to recognise that it isn't always the most expensive man for the job who is best. However deep your money-pool is, sometimes you don't have to dig very deeply into it to find the right coaches and trainers. Iran has spent a great deal of money in establishing football in Tehran and the provinces over the last decade, but the policy has never been to attempt a vast buying operation to permit them to play in the international stadiums. However, one must remember that in many cases boys with talent, scooped up from the provinces, are what we might term 'hungry players', and the very idea of having their own kit and spending money gives them a great appetite for the game. Their aptitude is comparable

In football you cannot buy success without the intelligence to recognise that it isn't always the most expensive man for the job who is best

to that of the Brazilians and they have a definite advantage over other Asian countries. Add to this the fact that they know the Shah has a real interest in the game – his son, Crown Prince Reza, has his own team in the palace grounds – and it comes as no surprise that the young and talented footballers of Iran feel encouraged in every way to work hard at their game and have pride in their country's national sport.

At the beginning of the present decade, Iran thought in terms of developing and streamlining its football. The national team had already shown encouraging signs and had won the 1968 Asian Cup competition; 1972 saw them with the Asian Cup again. By 1975 there was a national league: the first division consists of sixteen teams and there is now a successful second division. Overall there are some four hundred clubs in Iran with two thousand teams and forty-three thousand players. With the Iranian FA's encouragement several leading clubs have foreign trainers and coaches, Russian and Yugoslavians as well as Europeans. Most of the top teams come from the capital Tehran, whilst Tabriz and Abadan are also well represented.

A great deal of thought has gone into the planning and aims of Iranian football. The grass roots of the game, youth, are well taken care of, and a national youth team has been in operation for some time. Many youth and senior tournaments have been organised and hosted by Iran, with an ever-watchful eye on developments in visiting national teams' tactics and approach to the game.

Shortly after Iran's failure to reach Munich in 1974, Frank O'Farrell was approached and asked to take charge of the national team. This was a choice that met with much approval from the knowledgeable football bastions – a highly respected British manager who had achieved a great deal in his homeland and had just parted with Manchester United. His assistant was Hechmat Mohadjerani, and Jack Skinner, another English coach, was in charge of national youth football. The Asian Cup was won for a third time in 1976 – no mean feat, for Asia is a vast and varied footballing continent – and in the same year Iran reached the final stages of the Olympics. When

Facing page: Coach Frank O'Farrell and his successful team pose with Crown Prince Reza after winning the Asian Cup for the third time in 1976. His legacy is still strong in Iran.

O'Farrell left at the end of his two-year appointment Mohadjerani took over the reigns and continued with the work that had already been achieved. The Iranian FA seemed to be following the excellent example of the West Germans, who always have a man who has worked with and assisted the retiring national team manager groomed and ready to take over.

Mohadjerani has taken charge of a national team which has enjoyed increasing success under his guidance. The country's outstanding player at present is thirty-year-old midfield general Ali Parvin, who has made fifty appearances for his country and captained the 1976 Olympic team. Team manager and captain have a great understanding and a deep respect for each other. Other talented players to watch for are Hejazi, their goalkeeper, Gosampur, another midfield motivator, Mazoulmi, a forward and Roushan, who was Iran's match-winner in Australia, scoring an excellent goal.

The organisation of their World Cup squad must be the envy of many nations, for at least a month before qualifying matches the team is called together for extensive preparation. Mohadjerani has complete control of his players in a manner unknown to his colleagues across the world. All this is part of the excellent planning and thought put into the game by the Iranian Football Federation led by K. Attabah.

In June 1978 Iran will not arrive as the minnows of the World Cup finals. They will arrive convinced they are as good as any of the teams on show; they may not believe that they can lift gold straight away, but they do believe that they can play good and attractive football which will please not just their audience but themselves as well. They will not leave the sporting arena without leaving a definite mark, for they are a proud and determined race with a famous history, to which they would very much like to add a little modern colour.

Tunisia

This is a young country, led for the last two decades by Habib Bourguiba, an enormously popular President who is attempting to develop his nation at high speed and deal with its internal economic problems. In every corner of this African/Middle Eastern nation there are signs of redevelopment and improvement. Great efforts have and continue to be made to deal with education, unemployment, modernising

industry and keeping inflation at a reasonable level. There is a great attack being made on the tourist trade and holiday visitors are being pulled towards this country by a hot tanning sun, attractive beaches and some first-class hotels, though it is incongruous to still see children in rags living in broken-down huts at the foot of the Tunis Hilton Hotel.

The Tunisians are great lovers of football and support 164 national teams playing in four divisions. In 1956 the Federation of Tunisian Football was formed and the game was quickly put into order. The best possible administrators were found to deal with and organise the mushrooming clubs and the thousands of players registering to play for them. At the moment there are 14,400 authorised players playing throughout the four divisions, though not one of them is a full-time professional! They all, including the top players who represent the national team, work outside football to make a living. A large number of them work in banks or are representatives and salesmen in industry. There is a ready understanding with employers to secure time off with pay whenever employees are needed by clubs or the national team. The clubs themselves pay their players' expenses for travelling and a small bonus for a win.

Each club must, by the rules of the Federation, have on their playing staff 'pupils' aged between 11 to 12, 'minors' aged 13 to 19, 'cadets' aged 15 to 16, 'juniors' aged 17 to 18, 'junior seniors' aged 19 to 20 and finally the 'senior' players who are 21 and over. A club cannot operate unless it contains players in all five categories leading up to the seniors. Players are cared for on a professional basis, including being given first-class medical attention and guidance and help in work outside the game. The men and boys play for 14 national clubs in what we would call the 'super league', 24 clubs in division two and 72 and 54 clubs in divisions three and four respectively.

The system to find champions and relegation candidates are a little complicated outside the 'super league', where one club wins the title and two are relegated to the second division. In this second division the clubs are split into north and south, twelve

Far left: Junior World Cup display in El Menzah stadium.
Below: Official poster for the tournament.
Centre: Attouga, 'The Chicken', the hero of the Tunisian national team. It is rare indeed for a goalkeeper to captain a team at any level, let alone his country's World Cup side.

TOURNOI MONDIAL JUNIORS DE LA FIFA DOTE DU CHALLENGE COCA-COLA

TUNIS '77

27 JUIN - 10 JUILLET

in each area playing for promotion and to avoid relegation. At the end of the season northern and southern champions join the 'super league' and two clubs fall into the third division. The third division holds some 72 clubs and is split into seven separate divisions. The winners of each division play each other at season's end to find the champions and runners-up. The two clubs with the worst records for the season go down into the fourth division which holds fifty-four clubs and promotes two each season. As well as this long league programme there are many cup competitions, the most important being the 'Coupe de Tunisie', the competition open to all clubs on a knock-out basis, the winners collecting the 'Bourguiba Cup'. Then there are cup competitions for all the different classes of players – pupils, minors, cadets and so on.

The gate money from league matches gives the competing clubs 50% of the collected revenue, three-quarters to the home team and one-quarter to the visitors. The other 50% is made up as follows:

3% tax	11% Ministry of Sport
1% insurance	10% stadium fees (few teams have their own)
4% Football Federation	4% officials
4% police	13% referee and linesmen

Cup matches vary somewhat, giving the teams a larger slice of the profits.

In a country containing so many clubs, there are surprisingly only 50 stadiums to play in and only seven top clubs have their own. These clubs can only run them by being connected to industry and receiving sponsorship in return. In consequence much sharing of amenities is arranged which helps the lower and poorer clubs' continued survival. In a struggling economic climate such arrangements work well and perhaps there is a lesson to be learned by many European countries here. Out of the fifty stadiums only two outside Tunis, Sousse and Sfax, have grass pitches, though now more are being prepared. The rest have hard sandy surfaces.

This is the background to the development of some very talented club and international players. As individuals and teams they can also conduct themselves in a very sporting manner. A strong reason for this must be the firm strictures of Tunisian refereeing. Men in this capacity have, since 1972, gone through rigorous training in all aspects of the game, including legislation and medicine, and they must have played football for at least two years for a club. The average age for a referee is 28 and he must retire at 45. At the present time there are some 427 officials yet only 45 are in the top bracket. Five of these are qualified to referee internationals. They are in a select group termed the *Federaux*.

In recent years the star name associated with Tunisian football – and a player who has been seen as a leading world-class goalkeeper – is Sassi Sadok, better known by his nickname Attouga. There are many stories of how he came by this name, which means chicken, but it certainly has nothing to do with

his lack of heroics in the goalmouth. Possibly it stems from the crouching position he takes before springing into action, his body arched and his legs apart, as if he is about to lay an egg!

Here is a player who is idolised by the Tunisian football fan, especially the supporters of Club Africain de Tunis, his home team. He has been through the system in full, winning championship and cup medals and representing his country internationally, most recently in the successful preliminary rounds to qualify for the 1978 World Cup. Though he is captain of the Tunisian national team, he still remains an amateur, working as a sales representative for Coca-Cola to earn a living. His life-style is very moderate, and he lives with his wife and baby daughter in a small and ordinary home in an area close to Tunis. At 32, near the end of his career, here is a star who will have seen little financial return from a colourful career. Yet within the system he is perfectly happy.

Other names around him in the national team are Temime, of Espena Sportive de Tunis, a winger with an explosive scoring right foot; Akid, the tall and powerful centre-forward with exceptional heading ability; Agrebi and Tarek, two inside-forwards of surprising speed and talent. But Attouga towers above them all in first-class performances in match

Above: Pre-match tension builds up in the 100,000 seater Teheran stadium before Iran's 1977 qualifier against Kuwait. 135,000 (!) saw Iran win 1-0.

after match. His discipline and organisation on the pitch never falter and they are combined with a showman's desire to entertain – he even has a say in team selection. This man and his fellow-internationals are excellent advertisements for the game, encouragement to the young football addicts of Tunisia and useful emissaries for spreading the word visibly across the world that this young football nation is rapidly coming of age.

FIFA's World Youth Tournament 1977

On 27 June 1977, at the opening of the first ever World Youth Tournament in Tunis at the ultra modern, superbly equipped cantilevered El Menzah stadium, FIFA's President Joao Havelange said in his opening address:

'I see before me young people from all parts of the world drawn by the ideal of fair play, guided by feelings of brotherhood which overcome all considerations of race, religion or politics. They have come

> ‘Though captain of the Tunisian national team, he still remains an amateur, working as a sales representative for Coca-Cola to earn a living’

drawn by the magic attraction of sport which is one of the most important factors in the development of peace amongst all men . . . I am happy to see that under my Presidency FIFA has been able to organise this event against the welcoming background of Tunis, a young country too, also engaged in the development of a great future . . . by the enthusiastic support of the Government in Tunis which, under the direction of His Excellency Mr Habib Bourguiba, has spared no efforts so that the first World Youth Tournament which is taking place in this country was able to count on all the necessary elements for the total success of this project . . . and again the Coca-Cola company which enabled this tournament to be carried out . . .'

So with Tunisia as keen hosts, FIFA's foresight under Rous and later Havelange to start such a tournament and Coca-Cola's sponsorship – 1.6 million to be spread over four such tournaments, with dollars in reserve to be used if and when necessary – the planning was complete and the tournament could commence.

A Happy Surprise—and a Surfeit of Penalties

Sixteen nations including the hosts competed for two rewards, the Coca-Cola Cup and the Bourguiba Statuette. Brazil, Russia and Uruguay, of the 16 qualifying nations, were strongly fancied from the start and much was hoped for from the Tunisian team. No player born before 1959 was eligible to play for his country and all players would one day hope to compete in the World Cup – here was the cream of many nations' footballing youth.

The sixteen teams were split up into four groups, all playing on grass in the four best stadiums. The favourites marched steadily through their matches, with Mexico doing surprisingly well. Tunisia fell apart in their first two matches; Mexico hammered six past them, and France beat them one-nil. Brazil knocked five past the Iranian defence and were dancing to the semi-finals. Russia, who had arrived three weeks before the tournament began to acclimatise and prepare, marched strongly and impressively forward. Uruguay, a fine example of physical fitness, brushed all opposition aside. Russia, Mexico, Uruguay and Brazil reached the semi-finals.

The first, held in the evening heat of the El Menzah stadium, was Brazil against Mexico. Brazil had talent in depth, a young team playing in the style of their elders. Their number sixteen, Braslia, a substitute for an injured first choice, was a winger who had already electrified the crowds with his quicksilver talent and powerful shooting and was to be named best player of the tournament. However, this was not to be Brazil's best match. They attacked continuously, sending the Mexicans rocking back on their heels to defend desperately, a role that until now they had been unused to. But Brazil could not penetrate sufficiently, the Mexicans would not tire and at full-time it was one goal apiece. With no extra time allocated in the semi-finals, the overjoyed Mexicans won 5-3 on penalties. It was sad to see Brazil exit after dominating this semi-final and continuing their attacking style, but for the crowd Mexico were a good consolation prize as they had proved earlier that they too preferred to attack. Each player was

Below: FIFA-organised experimental game in Tunisia, testing kick- (rather than throw-) ins and short corners from the edge of the penalty area. Though largely unknown to the general public, games like these could eventually reshape certain aspects of football.
Above: Uruguayan radio commentator at the Junior World Cup semi-final between Uruguay and Russia.
Facing page: A defender from Russia's senior team challenges Argentina's Houseman during a previous international match.

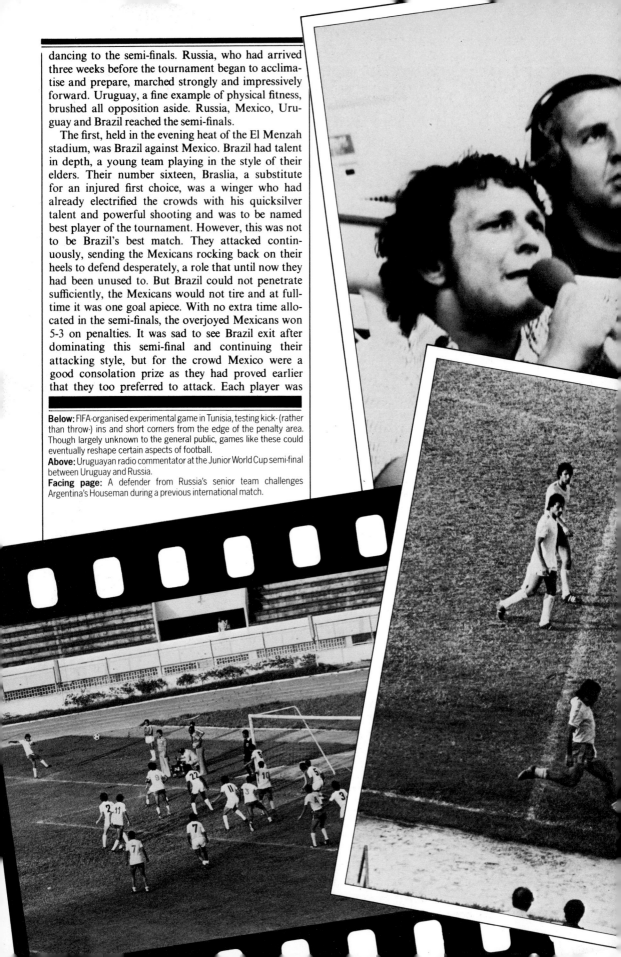

allowed to play his own game, and emphasis lay on individual skill within a team framework.

The following night saw the meeting of the two iron teams in the second semi-final: the impeccably organised Russians against the immensely fit Uruguayans. Perhaps not surprisingly, it turned out to be a dour match using planned defensive football, with the first shot coming after 37 minutes! The second half opened up a little, but at full-time it was stalemate. Neither defence had been stretched and the match had been dominated by midfield play, although the Russian attack had shown flashes of excitement, from Bessenov and Petrakov in particular. Again penalty kicks decided which team was to enter the final: after Russia had scored with their last kick they led 4-3, but before the tense crowd Uruguay missed their last kick.

Whilst Mexico and Russia waited for the final of the *Tournei Mondial Juniors*, the play-off between Brazil and Uruguay was staged. Brazil completely overran the surprisingly tired-looking Uruguayans, crushing them 4-0. The young Brazilians sparkled, none more so than Brasilia, though he left the scoring to his team-mates. Could the best team have come third?

The final arrived, with the fervent hope that it would be a true showcase of the world's two top youth teams. The referee was the 32-year-old Frenchman Vautrot, who had been highly assessed by FIFA in previous games in the tournament. His linesmen were the experienced referees Coelmo of Brazil and El Hawary of Egypt. There would be no communication problems, since French was understood by all three.

At first, tension was creating some messy football. But after 15 minutes the Russians started to move amazingly quickly and to string penetrating attacks together whilst the Mexicans were valiantly holding on.

Within two minutes of the restart Bessonov of Russia scored a fine goal. Within eight minutes Mexico equalised with a rocketing shot by Fernando from a direct free kick within the penalty box. Four minutes later Bessonov put Russia ahead again, powering home his second goal into the right-hand corner of the net. Watching this player reminded

enthusiasts at times of Cruyff. But Mexico wouldn't lie down; they accelerated their precise attacking play and four minutes later had equalised again from a low rasping shot by their whippet-like inside-forward Augustin. In the remaining 22 minutes, both teams played with energy to spare and continued to excite. Unfortunately Alvarez of Mexico was sent off for a late and over-vigorous tackle ten minutes from the end, but the ten Mexicans survived the final Russian onslaught.

Extra time was played in the final. Adrenalin was found to pump through twenty-one weary players, but no goals could be scored to decide the victors. So penalty kicks would have to decide the issue once more. In preparation, Russia brought on their substitute goal-keeper again a few minutes before the end of extra-time.

Nobody in that stadium wanted a result. If a show of hands had been asked, Russia and Mexico would have shared the Cup as they had shared the playing honours. Fate didn't seem to want a result either, and a second round of five penalties had to be taken under the stadium floodlights. Four goals each were scored,

Facing page: Tension shows as FIFA World Cup referee N'Daiye and Brazil and Mexico players watch the sudden-death penalties in their Junior semi-final.
Above: Action from the other semi-final, Uruguay versus Russia.
Centre: Dr. Jaoa Havelange, the new President of FIFA, is presented with the Coca-Cola Youth Cup in Tunisia before the semi-finals.

but Mexico pulled their fifth shot wide. If Russia scored from their last the championship was theirs; they did and Russia had won 11-10, brave and talented winners, with Mexico worthy and valiant runners-up.

It had been a successful tournament, with much good football, sporting play, good refereeing overall and an exciting marathon of a final.

The Future

After the Youth Tournament, what has Tunisia to look forward to now? Firstly a new season of football, when every Tunisian returns from afternoons on the beach to support fervently the large array of clubs. Children playing in the ruins of Carthage and the rugged hills find balls of old battered leather and

melted plastic and play with the dream of becoming a 'pupil'.

The biggest dream will be of Tunisia qualifying for Argentina in 1978. They have mastered the preliminary games and won through against Morocco, Algeria and Guinea. They must do battle now against their fellow group members, Zambia, Egypt and Nigeria. Should the Tunisians keep their nerve and play with their true talent, Argentina and the world audience for the finals will welcome this keen and young footballing nation. Whatever happens, unless the basic fibre of this country should change drastically in the years ahead, Tunisia, with its limited financial resources but immense keenness and application of talent within the game, will one day reach the finals of the World Cup.

The American Dream

It took the arrival in the USA of Pele, as a player and an ambassador of football, to convince the world that the game was actually being played there. The public relation boys made sure they gave what they term 'soccer' a good blast-off with newsreel shots of Pele having a kick-around with President Ford on the lawns of the White House. In football circles across the world there was a certain wry approval.

On arriving Pele was quoted as saying: 'When you throw a ball to a South American child he'll automatically trap it, throw it to an American child and he'll catch it'. The ambassador arrived on a dollar-packed contract, but knowing he had a mountain of a job to do. The North American Soccer League, with four nation-wide divisions of teams fighting for points to get them to the final of the 'play-off' (knock-out stage) for the Soccer Bowl Prize, needed Pele to spur on a soccer scene which was already well-organised, but suffering from anaemic support and a lack of top-line coaches. In an incredibly short time the wry approval had turned into enthusiasm, respect and delight from all quarters, and there is no one who can deny the possibility now of America dominating world football by the end of the next decade. Phil Woosnam, ex-West Ham, Aston Villa and England player and now NASL Commissioner, warned us of this, and now there is even the belief that America will win the World Cup before England does again.

Charging into the Soccer World

To go to a soccer match in Minnesota, Seattle, Portland, Tampa Bay, New York or Las Vegas is a totally new experience. America is supplying a nation with a high standard of living and big money to spend with leisure sports, of which 'Soccer' is the newest and fastest-growing. It is an incredible sight to see five thousand cars parked outside a stadium four hours before the kick-off – twenty thousand people there are having a great party and almost forgetting the reason for coming! A young woman breast-feeds her baby a few rows up from the touch-line. Top stars

Top: Copacabana Beach football in Rio de Janeiro. Many of Brazil's international stars were first spotted playing here.

Centre: As with the World Cup proper, FIFA's youth games attract dedicated spectators.

Below: Scratch team playing in the ruins of Carthage.

mix with paying public long before the match. The players run out on to artificial pitches, giving bouquets of flowers to women spectators, as a helicopter circles overhead and drops the match-ball on to the centre circle. Cheer-leaders drum up more excitement and atmosphere in the truly American tradition, electric scoreboards help to light up the fun as the progress of the game is accompanied by messages of support for the home team: 'Charge!' and 'Great goal'. Organ music is played as the match proceeds, very much in the 'silent movie' tradition with hero music, villain music, excitement music and happy music for a goal scored. Some players reckon the organ is worth a goal start in Tampa; the organ excites the crowd, the crowd atmosphere motivates the players and a goal results – to see all this fun is a real eye-opener. Fun is the first priority for the soccer promoters in the States; the game must be sold as entertainment. They must catch their spectators and then make sure they come back for more, and this they are doing. The second priority is improving coaching throughout the game with imported experts spreading their knowledge amongst the players and the hundreds who are interested in taking up similar work and developing the grass roots of the game within America's youth.

Soccer is being sold with a consumer-orientated approach. This is traditionally the way with sport in America; a family audience has always attended the major sports, and soccer has proved to be exactly the type of attraction a family can enjoy. Every stadium has seating throughout; there is no terracing and consequently no violence. All the PR work at the start was aimed at the kids and women, for youth is the basic foundation for future progress and if mom is happy to go to the game then the rest of the family is likely to follow suit.

Complete circuses have been used to entertain crowds before the match begins, followed by a high-wire act at half-time. This is total entertainment for the afternoon or early evening, and it spills over into the 90 minutes of soccer so that all ages of spectators are sharing mutual fun and not just observing. There is no black shadow of fear and violence hovering over American soccer, as it does in many parts of the world today. They are not yet playing to world class, but they are skilfully entertaining and at times giving exciting competitive exhibitions with the underlying message to the young that Gordon Hill, the respected English ex-referee who is now working as Director of Youth and Community Development for the Tampa Bay Rowdies, sums up as 'You haven't *got* to go out and win!'

This man is completely sold on the American attitude to developing the sport. The fear that is felt on European pitches will not be allowed to creep in. When and where a soccer club puts down its roots in a community, the club feels a responsibility to that community, and its member players, coaches and staff are seen to carry out that responsibility. People feel that the club is a big warm and generous friend and want to be part of the sporting activity. In return the club coaches the people in soccer, entertains splendidly and does invaluable charity work. The club is a good host and the community shares its

Complete circuses have been used to entertain crowds before the match begins, followed by a high-wire act at half-time

riches of organisation, experts and superstars who are no longer remote idols. For the clubs this is all good business sense, and for the paying public it is rewarding and enjoyable.

'Playing hockey I was always broke and banged up,' is a feeling expressed by a young American woman who enjoys sport but couldn't find a team game she really liked until soccer arrived. She goes on: 'Soccer is the best game in the world, you can play it all hours, I just need a ball and I can go out

and start a pick-up game: boys and girls, middle-aged women, even a 70-year-old guy join in'. This is a valid point, and communities all over the States are – like generations of young European and South American players before them – discovering the basic simplicity of the game in park or vacant lot, where all that is needed are some piles of clothing to make up the goal areas, a ball and from four to twenty-two people with energy and enthusiasm enough to play. Girls from five to fifty are playing, watching and enjoying the sport. Figures of attendance at soccer matches puts the female spectator as being between 48 and 60% of the crowd. The young woman interviewed earlier goes on:

'It's good for your body and builds stamina without muscles. Women now feel free to be competitive in a lot of sports, especially in soccer, as it's a team sport. It's mentally and emotionally good; without a release for competition you can screw up relationships and business, you can express yourself and your personality and still be a feminine competitor. We don't have to be either a toy doll or a truck-driver!'

Eusebio has been pleased to see soccer developing so well amongst women, though he has expressed worries about their bosoms! However, he needn't be so concerned, as a 'soccer bra' is being considered

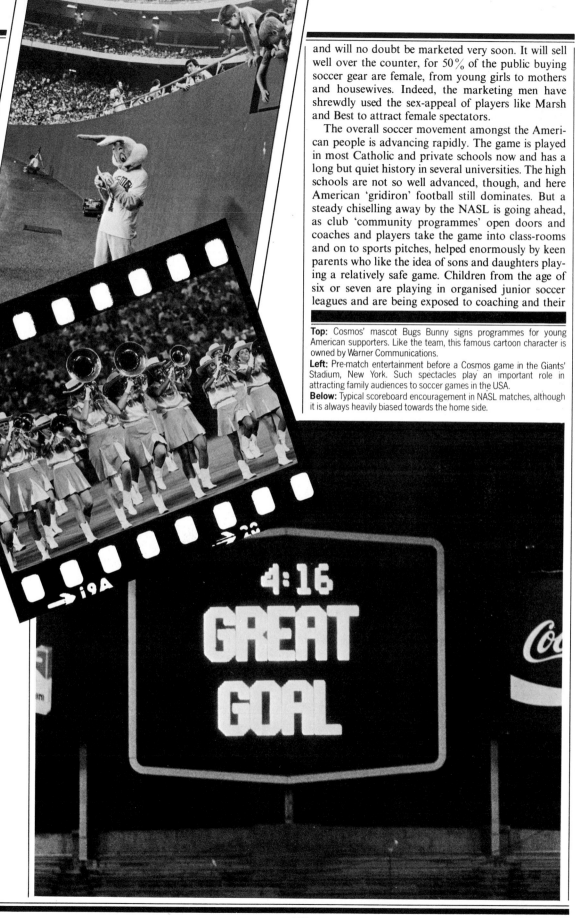

and will no doubt be marketed very soon. It will sell well over the counter, for 50% of the public buying soccer gear are female, from young girls to mothers and housewives. Indeed, the marketing men have shrewdly used the sex-appeal of players like Marsh and Best to attract female spectators.

The overall soccer movement amongst the American people is advancing rapidly. The game is played in most Catholic and private schools now and has a long but quiet history in several universities. The high schools are not so well advanced, though, and here American 'gridiron' football still dominates. But a steady chiselling away by the NASL is going ahead, as club 'community programmes' open doors and coaches and players take the game into class-rooms and on to sports pitches, helped enormously by keen parents who like the idea of sons and daughters playing a relatively safe game. Children from the age of six or seven are playing in organised junior soccer leagues and are being exposed to coaching and their

Top: Cosmos' mascot Bugs Bunny signs programmes for young American supporters. Like the team, this famous cartoon character is owned by Warner Communications.
Left: Pre-match entertainment before a Cosmos game in the Giants' Stadium, New York. Such spectacles play an important role in attracting family audiences to soccer games in the USA.
Below: Typical scoreboard encouragement in NASL matches, although it is always heavily biased towards the home side.

favourite stars in person. In the San José area of California where the Earthquakes play, eighty thousand youngsters alone are registered, of whom ten thousand are girls.

The professional players have a heavy and exacting career in American soccer. Their high wages require full-time devotion to the game for twelve months each year. For example, a soccer contract with Tampa Bay Rowdies generally obliges the player to assist in soccer clinics and training in schools, marketing the club on radio and television and at business conferences and Rotary Club lunches. For six months a player is contracted to play soccer, the other six to concentrate wholly on the public relations side, grass roots teaching and extensive charity work. The off-season in many ways is harder than the playing season! Players in general enjoy both sides of their work and in consequence develop a close, -friendly

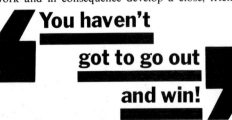

'You haven't got to go out and win!'

Above: Tampa Bay Rowdies mascot.
Facing page top: Russian players salute the Tunisian crowd after winning the Junior World Cup.
Facing page centre: Pele takes the field for his final NASL match, a game which won the Championship for Cosmos.

Facing page below right: Pele in the dressing room.
Facing page below left: Parade at a Cosmos game.
Following pages: International action from Holland-Belgium, Brazil-Poland (sequence) and Italy-Israel.

image with the public that admires and watches them on the pitch.

More and more players from all over the world are now being signed up on permanent contracts; the practice of short-term loans of players to America for the soccer season only seems to be over. The New York Cosmos spend up to three million dollars on players' salaries each year, although they don't always pay fortunes for buying a player. Some present soccer stars were bought for peanuts from second and third division teams in England, Italy, Brazil, Yugoslavia and other leading football nations. Gone are the days of seemingly crazy and extravagant buying, such as the American offer in the mid-sixties to buy the entire Wolverhampton Wanderers team and club lock, stock and barrel – the gold-shirted Wolves were playing and winning a summer soccer tournament in Los Angeles at the time of this extraordinary bid.

Gordon Hill, Tampa Bay Rowdies official

'I just need a ball and I can go out and start a pick-up game: boys and girls, middle-aged women, even a 70-year-old guy join in'

When the Americans do hit the headlines it is with a purpose and with a hard and precise eye on the future. Franz Beckenbauer was bought from the Bayern Munich club for a staggering £1,400,000; the size of the fee and the fact that the 'Kaiser' would now finish his playing career in America amazed the rest of the world. But for Beckenbauer, Pele, Best, Marsh, Moore and Eusebio the rewards are immense, and not just in terms of 'greenbacks'. Pele is quoted as saying, before his farewell match in New York when 76,000 people turned up at the Giants' stadium in New York to pay homage and bid farewell to the king of football: 'I hope I have given pleasure to some poor people around the world. I hope I have done something for Brazil. There have been times of serious political trouble in the country when football has made people happy and content. I feel I have helped bring soccer to the United States.' Indeed he

has; Warner Communications, who own the New York Cosmos as well as Bugs Bunny, Sylvester and Tweety Pie, Robert Redford and a host of other box-office attractions, were convinced he would start the soccer revolution in the USA. They will continue to employ Pele in public relations work, even though they could not persuade him to play on even for a reported £5.8 million offer. Cosmos now have Beckenbauer as the big attraction and there is no doubt that the chase for Cruyff is now under way.

Jeff Carter, the President's son, saw that Cosmos-Santos match. So too did Henry Kissinger, Muhammed Ali, Barbra Streisand, Mick Jagger, Robert Redford, along with countless current and former soccer internationals. In the first half Pele played for Cosmos and rifled home a free kick from 30 yards – his 1281st goal in 1365 games. In the second half he switched shirts and turned out for the last time as a Santos player once again. Although his old team went down 2-1, the result was of no importance; nobody wanted him to leave the pitch, nobody wanted those ninety minutes to end.

In memory of Pele, the No. 10 shirt that he made his own across the world will never again be worn by a Cosmos player. Just before that emotional game on Saturday, 1 October 1977, Pele remarked: 'I don't want people to think it will be the last time I ever kick a football. Soccer is my destiny. I will be teaching soccer, advising youngsters and giving clinics around the world. Part of me will die on Saturday. But

Facing page: 1977 World Cup qualifying match – Malta versus East Germany in austere surroundings. From teams like these – Turkey and Hong Kong, Bolivia and Egypt – dark horses emerge.

Below: Girls' soccer – as played here in California – has come a long way since the Lady Football Players of 1895 (see p13).

'Soccer is a kick in the grass'

Above: Australia is another developing nation, seen here in the 1974 World Cup games. Peter Wilson goes for the ball and (top) covers Branko Buljevic.

Facing page: Tunisian team and Iran's sports stadium.

don't feel sorry for me. I will still be involved in the game I love.'

Whilst the word 'booming' can be and is used to describe the development of soccer overall in the States, not every club is enjoying the upsurge. There are a few eking out a marginal existence and no one knows for sure the reason. The New York Cosmos, Tampa Bay Rowdies (slogan: 'Soccer is a kick in the grass'), Washington Diplomats, Portland and Minnesota can attract crowds of forty to fifty thousand. A 77,000 crowd watched Cosmos play Fort Lauderdale in 1977. Others, like the Las Vegas Quicksilvers and Los Angeles Aztecs, can only average home crowds of 6–12,000. Are they not doing enough advertising and public relations work or have they not attracted the right star players? Perhaps they are in areas where other leisure activities dominate – gambling in Las Vegas, the movie world in L.A. The

strong establishment of other sports – baseball and ice hockey for example – in the same city causes the Chicago soccer team to attract crowds as low as 98 spectators. Yet a move to New Jersey brought in crowds of 47–50,000 with a steady average of 25,000.

Excitement is the order of the day; attacking soccer is encouraged with an extra point for each of the first three goals on both sides and six points for a win. Purists would find the American game far too *consistently* exciting, especially with the 'sudden death' play-off to decide a drawn game. Two extra-time periods of seven and a half minutes are played and if a result is still not resolved the teams are allowed five shots at goal from 35 yards. Five different players take the shots and are allowed five seconds each to take the kick against the opposing goalkeeper.

Exploding scoreboards with fireworks, a shrinking offside area, Superman astride the stadium entrance, the Coca-Cola Youth Tournament, the 'Soccer Bowl', Cosmos' goalkeeper appearing in *Playgirl*, wide participation and education in youth soccer, a star player reprimanded for scoring a glorious goal during a TV commercial break – all this is America's soccer scene. It it also a common language for the mixture of races, and a way of knitting together the family unit with one common interest. America is through the soccer revolution and, marching forward with the support of young and old, is already producing home grown talent, and will continue to attract world-class players. A Cosmos official is quoted as saying 'It would blow your mind to learn the players who have told us they want to come here to play. It reads like a *Who's Who* of English football.' Even hopefuls playing in the shadows with small clubs around the world are praying for the chance to reach the big time in the USA. Given the opportunity, they feel that they can emulate the meteoric rise to fame of players like Steve Hunt of Cosmos. An unknown Aston Villa reserve in the early months of 1977, he was a Cosmos star at the end of the summer. He scored one goal and made another in their 2-1 NASL title play-off against Seattle Sounders and at only 21 is already idolised by the crowds, playing alongside the great names he once hero-worshipped and earning more in that one season than he could do in years in England. In that season he scored 14 goals, was credited with 16 'assists' and won 8 man-of-the-match awards. He now appears in TV commercials and has his own fan club: a far cry from Villa Park.

In the past players often went to America to finish their careers in clover, but young men like Hunt now see a real opportunity on the astroturf of America which they would never see on the endless round of bare, muddy third- and fourth-division pitches in England. Good coaching will always be available to maintain the impetus already given to the sport and to bring the dream of World Cup participation in the 1980s to fruition.

FIFA WORLD YOUTH TOURNAMENT FOR THE COCA-COLA CUP 1977

GROUP A
TUNIS-EL MENZAH

France 1, Spain 2 (HT 0/0)
Mexico 6, Tunisia 0 (HT 0/0)
Spain 1, Mexico 1 (HT 0/0
Tunisia 0, France 1 (HT 0/0)
France 1, Mexico 1 (HT 0/0)
Tunisia 1, Spain 0 (HT 0/0)

	P	W	D	L	F	A	Pts
Mexico	3	1	2	0	8	2	4
France	3	1	1	1	3	3	3
Spain	3	1	1	1	3	3	3
Tunisia	3	1	0	2	1	7	2

GROUP B
TUNIS-ZOUITEN

Morocco 0, Honduras 1 (HT 0/0)
Uruguay 2, Hungary 1 (HT 0/0)
Honduras 0, Uruguay 1 (HT 0/0)
Hungary 2, Morocco 0 (HT 0/0)
Uruguay 3, Morocco 0 (HT 0/0)
Honduras 2, Hungary 0 (HT 0/0)

	P	W	D	L	F	A	Pts
Uruguay	3	3	0	0	6	1	6
Honduras	3	2	0	1	3	1	4
Hungary	3	1	0	2	3	4	2
Morocco	3	0	0	3	0	8	0

GROUP C
SOUSSE

Italy 1, Ivory Coast 1 (HT 0/0)
Brazil 5, Iran 1 (HT 0/0)
Iran 0, Italy 0 (HT 0/0)
Ivory Coast 1, Brazil 1 (HT 0/0)
Iran 3, Ivory Coast 0 (HT 0/0)
Brazil 2, Italy 0 (HT 0/0)

	P	W	D	L	F	A	Pts
Brazil	3	2	1	0	8	2	5
Iran	3	1	1	1	4	5	3
Italy	3	0	2	1	1	3	2
Ivory Coast	3	0	2	1	2	5	2

GROUP D
SFAX

USSR 3, Irak 1 (HT 0/0)
Paraguay 1, Austria 0 (HT 0/0)
Irak 5, Austria 1 (HT 0/0)
Paraguay 1, USSR 2 (HT 0/0)
Paraguay 4, Irak 0 (HT 0/0)
USSR 0, Austria 0 (HT 0/0)

	P	W	D	L	F	A	Pts
USSR	3	2	1	0	5	2	5
Paraguay	3	2	0	1	6	2	4
Irak	3	1	0	2	6	8	2
Austria	3	0	1	2	1	6	1

SEMI-FINALS
TUNIS-EL MENZAH

Mexico 1, Brazil 1 (HT 0/0)
(Mexico won 5-3 on penalties.)
USSR 0, Uruguay 0 (HT 0/0)
(USSR won 4-3 on penalties.)
Third and Fourth Place: Brazil 4, Uruguay 0 (HT 0/0)

FINAL
TUNIS-EL MENZAH

Mexico 2, USSR 2 (HT 0/0)
(USSR won 9-8 on penalties.)

Chapter Five

THE SWEAT MERCHANTS

Take one strong-willed, intelligent man, add a talent for football and lace it with the ability to organise, select, reject, buy and sell other men. Throw in a necessary gift for psychology, psychiatry and leadership – and you have a football manager.

Football managers are the sweat merchants, the Svengalis of modern football. They take the cream of a nation's players and weld them into a winning team . . . or accept the frightening responsibility of failure on their shoulders alone. Before they even begin they must have these talents and more. Yet when it comes to the crunch, the manager must sit on the sideline and trust his players to speak for him through their skills and team-work.

When he has finished coaxing and cajoling his players, and has worked them up to key fitness and co-ordination levels as well as total understanding as a unit, he allows them to wash away the sweat under a shower . . . and then he goes away to sweat on his own. The most terrifying aspect of football management is that awesome gap between the touchline and the pitch when the game begins. No matter what he does or says, the manager is helpless, a true victim of his own doctrines, at the end of the day.

Few people realise that football management involves as much as it does. Many believe the job to be nothing more than a glorified trainer's role with tracksuit, whistle, press-ups, a few laps around a pitch and a game of five-a-side. This chapter will smash that myth forever. Because football managers are, truly, the sweat merchants.

Supremos of the Past

To illustrate the pressures, achievements, varied talents and weaknesses of great managers, we begin with a look at the most famous managers in international football history. The men who most merit attention are Vittorio Pozzo and Hugo Meisl of the 1930s, George Raynor and Sepp Herberger of the 1940s and 1950s, Alf Ramsey and Helmut Schoen of the 1960s and Schoen, Mario Zagalo and Rinus Michels of the 1970s. Each man faced very different problems. Factors such as the political climate of

Below: Mario Zagalo, Brazil's coach in 1974.
Right: Cesar Luis Menotti, Argentina's national manager for 1978, is on a hiding to nothing. At the moment he is trying to weld together a winning host team, in the knowledge that he must not be the first to let a visiting team win in South America.
Facing page top: The great Helmut Schoen of West Germany.
Facing page below: England players are put through their paces.

> ## They take the cream of a nation's players and weld them into a winning team . . . or accept the frightening weight of responsibility on their shoulders alone

their nations and their era played a big part. The growth of player-power took its toll in Holland. The changing systems within the game threatened to make successful managers history teachers overnight.

Few managers in modern football history experienced more political pressure than Vittorio Pozzo, Italy's *commissario tecnico* in the 1934 World Cup. A great authoritarian, he also became a revered father-figure to Italian football. Pozzo was shrewd, a good politician and an early-day football psychologist at a time when football managers were making the players and the ball do the work while they barked the orders.

One of his most successful ploys was his use of sleeping arrangements on away trips to crush internal arguments amongst his star players. Pozzo always made warring stars share the same room: the Juventus and Inter Milan *prima donnas* for example, players who often bickered away the hours – and their team's chances of success – through jealousy. By the time they realised they were sharing the same room, petty squabbles died away and a better understanding was struck up.

A small, sturdy man, Pozzo much admired the Manchester United team of that era and also studied in Switzerland before travelling to England. He fell in love with England and for a while refused to go home. But political life in Italy was simmering and soon soared towards the explosion of fascism under Benito Mussolini. With Italy's dictator using the World Cup as a political vehicle Pozzo was under an obvious pressure to make sure the home side triumphed. They did, beating Czechoslovakia 2-1 in the final. Four years later, Pozzo repeated his triumph in France when his *Azzurri* beat Hungary 4-2 in a tremendous final. What few people realise, however, is that with World War II breaking out, Italy were to hold the World Cup longer than any other country, for sixteen years from 1934 to 1950.

Pozzo's friend and fellow authoritarian was Hugo Meisl, who managed Austria in much the same way Pozzo managed Italy. Similar men in outlook, they both shared a third-part friendship . . . with the legendary Herbert Chapman of Arsenal.

Birds of a football feather, they gave football an extra dimension by way of their ability to communicate with their players outside training sessions. Meisl, however, never touched the heights achieved by Pozzo. But then he did not have players of the same quality at his disposal, and the German political machine was rumbling louder and louder through his most influential years. Political climate was Meisl's biggest drawback.

So much has been written about Brazil's magical presence in the 1958 World Cup in Sweden that the host nation's manager is often forgotten. We have already seen how, from being reserve team trainer at Aldershot in 1946, George Raynor was catapulted to the position of manager of the Swedish national team. The players loved him and he guided them to the Olympic gold medal in 1948. Italian clubs swooped to snatch four of his best players, but Raynor rebuilt his team with characteristic speed in time to give Brazil the fright of their lives in the World Cup Final. Sadly, when he returned to England, Raynor found coaching on a comparable level hard to come by, apart from brief spells as manager with Skegness and Doncaster Rovers. He spent time working in a holiday camp but is now, at the age of 71, President of the Doncaster and District Association of Football Coaches and deeply involved in encouraging football's grass roots. With numerous titles bestowed on him by Queen Elizabeth II, the King of Sweden and others, he is now listed in the *Guinness Book of Records* as the most successful national coach in the world.

The West German team of 1954 owed its unique style to one man – Sepp Herberger. He had the personality and power to make his players give more than they knew they had. They worked hard all the time, never allowing opponents to build up momentum. Fit and disciplined, the Germans crept from the ashes of a Second World War disaster to become world champions.

Herberger's immense air of authority and confidence gave his players an extra lift, but he also made sure their physical preparation left them lacking in no departments. When they had the ball, they were able to maintain what was then a very fast pace of play. Their tempo – set by Herberger – certainly swept red-hot favourites Hungary aside in the 1954 final, despite the fact that the Hungarians took a 2-0 lead early in the first half.

Following closely in the footsteps of these great men were many young managers who also achieved levels of success within their own nations. But few of them survived eras of change and political pressures.

The Great Managers of the Sixties

Sir Alf Ramsey, or Alf as he was known during most of his reign, guided little Ipswich Town to Second

Top: George Raynor, according to the Guinness Book of Records the most successful national manager in history, took Sweden to the final in 1958.
Left: Italy's Pozzo in Paris for the 1938 World Cup. His close emotional ties with his players virtually guaranteed success.

Division and First Division titles in the early 1960s. He succeeded Walter Winterbottom as England manager, and on 27 February, 1963 he sent England out for their first game under his rule. His reign ended in 1 March, 1974 when the FA wielded the axe over their world-famous knight. In eleven years, Ramsey led England through 113 games of which only 17 were lost – a truly remarkable record.

The Ramsey era had a great effect on English football. He altered the balance of power within the FA and had a lot to do with the end of amateurism. Ramsey gave the England manager's job a new image, and earned the respect of players and administrators alike. Unfortunately, he had little time for the outside world, least of all the media, and therefore had to suffer the abuse which resulted from their frustration at failing to break through the Ramsey barrier of communication.

His thoroughness of preparation and his considerable tactical knowledge gave the England team a new look also. But Ramsey did have the distinct advantage of taking control at a time when a new group of world-class players were emerging from domestic football. Around men such as Bobby Moore, Gordon Banks, George Cohen, Bobby Charlton and Alan Ball Ramsey built his team; a team which would go on to win the 1966 World Cup. The wingless style of play he adopted as the blueprint for success had many critics, even when the World Cup was won. But Ramsey was astute enough to make the best of his players' strengths, and it paid off.

Ramsey's greatest asset was the loyalty of his players. The reason for this was his loyalty to them. He refused to criticise his players in public, left them to enjoy the fruits of success and emerged only to accept the burden of defeat on his own shoulders.

Perhaps his major error was an excess of loyalty. For too long he attempted to keep together those players who had served him best, and the England team grew old together. Yet they came within an inch of reaching the World Cup semi-finals four years later in Leon, Mexico. But this time, West Germany extracted revenge for the 1966 defeat by winning 3-2. England's failure in Mexico marked the beginning of the end of Ramsey's era. When West Germany again spiked his guns in the 1972 European Championship the press began howling for blood – Ramsey's blood. His last two years as England manager – which were by no means unsuccessful in terms of results – were conducted in the face of an increasing barrage of criticism from the press.

A remarkable man, he was born in the working-class suburbs of Dagenham, East London, yet his clipped speech reminded one of a former public school boy – but then dignity was always high on Ramsey's list of priorities. He went to the trouble of taking elocution lessons and quickly put his new clipped verse to the test by getting rid of the long-standing selection committee which had dogged Walter Winterbottom during his spell as manager. When Ramsey finally stepped out of the England manager's job, he did so with the style and dignity which had marked his long and historic reign. Not for him was there any back-biting, story-telling or bitter attacks on his 'enemies'. He simply thanked his players for their loyalty one by one, and turned his back on an England team which was never as successful before he took over and has never since touched his level of success.

Meanwhile, England's 3-2 defeat by West Germany back in 1970 had paved the way for Brazil to enter a new era, under a new manager who guided them to a crushing victory over the ultra-defensive Italians in a remarkable final.

Below left: Sir Alf Ramsey, Mexico 1970. In this World Cup his team probably played their most attractive football ever.
Below right and facing page top: Helmut Schoen on the bench and with the World Cup in 1974.
Facing page below left: The West German team training in Rio, 1977.
Facing page below right: Beckenbauer in training.

Mario Lobo Zagalo, former Brazilian World Cup winger, succeeded Joao Saldanha who had been sacked shortly before the 1970 finals because he contemplated dropping Pele! Zagalo used Pele, a brilliant young left-winger called Roberto Rivelino, Tostao, Gerson, Carlos Alberto and Jairzinhio, who scored in every round of the competition including the final. Brazil's football was a feast of attacking thrills, and for Zagalo victory brought an incredible World Cup 'treble'. He had played himself in the 1958 and 1962 winning teams, and had gone on to lead his country to victory after being in charge only for a matter of weeks.

While Ramsey and Zagalo were establishing their reputations, a former bank clerk and industrial foreign correspondent was quietly building an international managerial career which will not be bettered for many a decade. Helmut Schoen has done more for German football than any man, either before or after the Second World War. His country is eternally in Schoen's debt, and a detailed breakdown of his life and career will prove that point beyond doubt. Born on 15 September, 1915, Schoen was brought up in a middle-class background. His father was an art dealer and Helmut proved to be an intelligent child with a sharp mind and a talent for playing football. Eventually he joined Dresdner SC, with whom he won two League Championship medals and two Cup winners medals. A fact not generally known is that Schoen won 16 international caps for Germany between 1937 and 1941, scoring 17 goals from inside-forward.

Professional football had not then reached Germany, however, and therefore Schoen was able to put both of his considerable talents to use. He studied banking for a number of years before becoming a foreign correspondent. During his travels he picked up a conversational knowledge of English and French, great assets to him in later years when he became manager of West Germany.

When his playing career ended he became coach to SV Wiesbaden before moving on to become assistant

Helmut Schoen

Facing page top: Eddie Firmani, a player and manager in the UK, now manager of the New York Cosmos.

Facing page below: Jack and Bobby Charlton (in Mexico for the 1970 World Cup) are two more famous players who made the move into management.

Above: But out on the pitch, a manager can only watch his players dictate his team's destiny.

'The team must be convinced that the boss is correct'

to the national team manager – the great Sepp Herberger – in 1956. One can only speculate as to how much Herberger influenced the young Schoen. But one thing is certain: the pupil emulated the master exactly 20 years after the latter's greatest triumph. Herberger guided West Germany to World Cup success in 1954 and Schoen, after leading his nation to the runners-up spot in 1966 and third place in 1970, won the World Cup, in West Germany, in 1974.

In between he won the European Championship in 1972 when West Germany crushed Russia 3-0 in the final. Some say the shadow of the legendary Herberger is that cast by Schoen in the sundown hours. Certainly

something has persuaded Schoen, who has seen everything and done everything a national manager can do, to carry on and lead West Germany to Argentina as holders. Whatever happens, he cannot end his career as anything other than a national hero – if not a football institution. Schoen is already a legend in his own time, but that tells little of the man or his character.

Herberger retired after 28 years as manager, and

'Any playing systems are only useful if they fit the players available'

there was no question as to the name of his successor. Eight years after taking the job of assistant national coach, Helmut Schoen became manager of his country. An era had begun – an era still stretching itself beyond the limits of any expectations. He knew the players but he did not deliberately set out to emulate Herberger. 'Copies are never as good as the original product,' says Schoen, a statement which instantly reminds one of his father's art dealings.

From the beginning Schoen made his own job easy. He made sure he had a press officer available to handle the media. He hates loaded questions and appears hyper-sensitive when tackled with something which he considers to be loaded. But unlike the blunt Ramsey, Schoen took steps to protect himself from creating what could become a damaging image. A press officer kept the media happy while Schoen got on with his job. Even when he went to Mexico in 1970, a special press officer was appointed. Thus the Germans became popular for their apparent openness to the press while Ramsey's England took unmerciful criticism because of their manager's off-hand manner and cold exterior.

Schoen's football philosophy is based on the central European school of football, which places ball control and artistry above speed and physical prowess. As we have established, Schoen was a player of considerable skill and cunning; without doubt this explains why he prefers players endowed with talent rather than willing workhorses. During his reign Schoen has capped players such as Seeler, Beckenbauer, Muller, Overath, Breitner, Hoeness, Netzer, Grabowski, Haller, Heynckes, Bonhof and Holzenbein – all players of individual skill.

Ironically, despite his love for skill and flair, Schoen was initially a cautious manager with a reputation for careful preparation which allowed for few risks. Over the years, and mellowed by the glow of success, Schoen has relaxed this tight approach, though in his book *Always on the Ball* he does say:

'One must prepare scrupulously and convince the players that the correct selection has been made. The candidates for the team should also be quite willing to accept their duties inwardly. I believe that herein lies one of the principal responsibilities of a manager. The team must be convinced that the boss is correct to such an extent that each player should feel that he would have made the same plans and decisions if he were manager. . . . Any playing systems are only useful if they fit the players available and if they can be turned into practice on the field of play. It is pointless indulging in special plans or methods, no matter how clever or cunning, if the players are not at one's disposal.'

Schoen has a good way with players. His philosophy concerning young players would serve many other managers, sometimes panic prone and impatient, very well: 'A young player must be carefully nursed and allowed one, two or even three poor games. It does not matter as long as one is convinced of the young player's talent.'

To be fair to other managers, however, Schoen has also had the kind of support given to Ramsey in that his reign has coincided with a period when West German domestic football has produced some world-class players. Schoen has also had a top-class club side to draw on in Bayern Munich, whose key players – Muller, Beckenbauer, Schwarzenbeck and Maier – provided the backbone of the national team. A significant sign of changing times, however, is that mighty Bayern are on the wane. Muller is close to retirement, Maier is getting on, Beckenbauer has gone to the United States and the West German team which played the second half of their international against Yugoslavia in Belgrade this year did not have one Bayern player in its line-up.

Nevertheless, the cool and brilliant organisational powers of Schoen have already coped with this problem of changing faces and the need to rebuild West Germany. With 19 months to the Argentina finals, Schoen had arranged no less than 18 international fixtures, as well as 14 'B' fixtures – trial internationals in which he bloods the absolute newcomers against nations such as Norway, Denmark and Eire. Watching the progress of all young players along with Schoen will be new national captain, Bertie Vogts, a totally different character to the aloof Beckenbauer, but a respected and talented captain just the same. By January 1978, Schoen will have named a squad of 40 players for the World Cup Finals. Each player will have regular medical checks and form checks until the time comes to reduce the squad to the 22 international players who will travel to South America.

There is no doubt that Schoen wanted to retire after winning the World Cup in 1974. He was persuaded to stay on. He has already built another team around some of the young bloods who came to the fore in 1974 and who now are showing their full powers, as well as several new and exciting faces. Whatever they might achieve, Schoen and the earlier West German teams have already done better. And in typical style, just as he succeeded Herberger, Schoen knows now who will take his place as national manager after 1978 – current 'B' team manager Jupp Derwall, who has been with Schoen for many years.

Helmut Schoen is undoubtedly one of the true sweat merchants. He is discreet, astute and experienced enough to keep his deep emotions to himself and exactly how much he suffered after the 1966 and 1970 disappointments will never be known. What mental

Top: Roberto of Brazil, one of the new superstars. His skill as a striker is already proven on the international scene.
Below: Mexico (in green) play El Salvador in a 1977 qualifying match.

'I consider him too indisciplined for football'

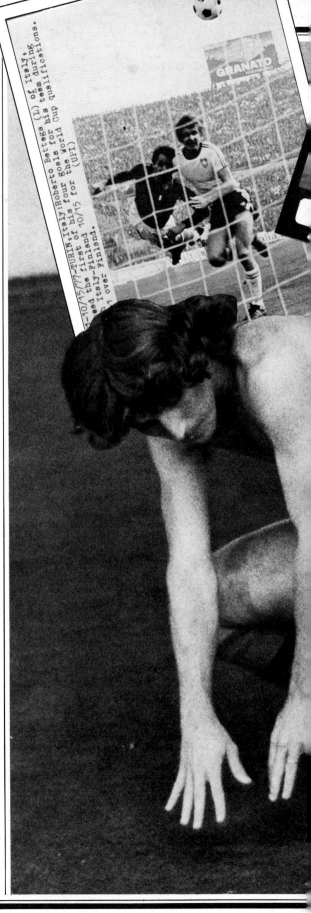

agonies he endured during the 1974 series on his own soil can only be imagined. Now, at least, he goes to South America more relaxed than any other manager who will be there.

Today's Managers

The same cannot be said for Brazil's latest manager, Claudio Coutinho, who has seen his new-look team safely into the finals. A brief glance back through the history of Brazilian managers will reveal that, for every triumphant manager behind a World Cup-winning team, there was a sacked manager who came within months of fulfilling his work before being axed.

Oswaldo Brando must hold an all-time world record for having the best managerial record prior to being sacked. In the second half of his 22-game reign Brazil recorded 12 wins and a 0-0 draw. It was the draw – against lowly Colombia – that sent the press for his throat. And in Brazil, public pressure counts for a lot, not to mention the extraordinary political problems which face every national supremo. When you consider that the 0-0 result was labelled 'a major disaster' one can only guess at the reaction to a 2-1 home win over Finland and home defeats by Wales and Scotland.

Brando simply did not know how to handle the political games of Brazilian football. For example, he announced that Francisco Marinho – 'I consider him too indisciplined for football,' he said – would never play for Brazil again . . . and made this statement two days before the ill-fated Colombia match. The public reaction was one of rampant fury, because the young defender is one of the few Brazilian footballers admired in every one of the fiercely partisan states. One of the national manager's most onerous tasks is to try and placate all the states at the same time.

The press screamed for changes. It arrived in the shape of a tall, handsome ex-army captain, 37-year-old Claudio Coutinho. Oddly enough, Coutinho's major honours were won at volleyball, but he is admired as a fierce advocate of total football with the accent on flair, skills and attack.

Manager of Flamengo, he also had had earlier experience with the national team, acting as physical trainer to the unforgettable 1970 side. He also speaks four languages – English, French, Spanish and of course Portuguese. And Coutinho adds realism to his obvious talents; of his predecessor Brando he says: 'He lost only one match out of 22 and was forced to resign.' Perhaps it is this awesome responsibility that

Top left: Roberto Bettega, Italy's feared striker.
Top right: Enzo Bearzot, Italy's manager, outside the River Plate stadium in Argentina.
Below: Zico of Brazil, to many the new Pele.

"We have never won the World Cup, yet we have the best players in the world"

Cesar Luis Menotti, Argentinian manager

causes him to add: 'I am 37, but such is the strain that I will be 50 next year!'

Brando himself hits the nail more firmly and accurately:

'It is generally accepted that unpopular team selections cost me my job. The Brazilian press is always looking for a scapegoat. I was the obvious choice.

'In Brazil the cities of Rio and Sao Paulo are traditionally the most powerful. But since the National Championship was brought in teams from others states have come to the fore.

'If the national manager selects a player, he not only has to be certain of the man's playing pedigree but also ensure that the man is politically acceptable. It sometimes reaches the incredible and frightening stage where the exclusion of certain players from certain provinces leads to something akin to a civil war.

'My folly was not selecting enough players from Rio. As a result the whole city turned against me. I have left Claudio Coutinho a well-framed team. I wish him well.'

In a country where football is next to religion, the manager of the national team experiences pressures which European managers simply would not tolerate. Despite this strain, Coutinho is brave enough to say his piece and stand by his judgement. Of Argentina he says:

'They are standing still where we are modernising our football. Their manager, Cesar Menotti is a traditional-ist who believes only in the superior ability of the South American footballer.

'I may agree with his belief in our basic skills, but we must also keep pace with the rest of the world.'

By this Coutinho means keeping a close watch on European football. He is a fanatical student of English coaching methods and of the FA coaching manuals.

Brazil is a unique football nation – a nation of the three s's . . . soccer, sex and samba in that order of importance. Governments totter and priorities change if the national team falls below the standards of the other two. This is why Claudio Coutinho is a sweat merchant with a difference – he carries a nation on his back.

Managing Argentina

So with West Germany and Brazil safely qualified and now in full swing with practice matches, what of

❝ Sometimes all the responsibility frightens me. I am really scared of disappointing my people ❞

Cesar Luis Menotti

the host nation herself? Who really knows what awaits the unsuspecting football world in 1978? Argentina is a country of fierce political passions, a land where political extremists, priests, old women, children and armed soldiers share the same sun-baked pavements.

But for all this, Argentina wants the World Cup. They want to stage the competition and then become the fifth host country to win it. A lot of national prestige is at stake, and apart from a few moments when natural instincts overcame restraint and boots and fists flew, the national team is fighting to establish a new image – one of skill, rather than the image Ramsey gave them.

The man who is on a massive hiding to nothing is Cesar Luis Menotti, national manager, defender of the South American faith and the man most likely to see heaven before all of us if Argentina fail. Menotti is a former Huracan player whose chief claim to fame so far is his bold announcement: 'We have never won the World Cup, yet we have the best players in the world.' Argentina have reached World Cup semi-finals and a final. The players' natural skills are not questioned; their temperaments and attitude towards football are.

What is easily forgotten is that Menotti has had three years of solid preparation. Their European tour in 1976 was highlighted by victories over Poland and Russia – no mean feats. Yet Menotti is aware of Argentina's biggest failing:

'Our ball control is fantastic and our game tends to be slow because the players enjoy holding the ball, feeling it and displaying their skills. But they hold the ball too long before passing it and this is where we must improve if we are to cope with European teams.'

One of the equally crippling problems is the number of star players who leave every year for Europe, big money and often their spiritual home, Spain. Menotti has already made up his mind to rely on home-based players. Perhaps he will include one or two exiles, but he is too aware of the dangers of relying on players coming back from Europe – players he has neither seen nor worked with for many months.

His record in 1976 was average-to-good by Argentinian standards: eight games won, three drawn,

four lost. By Brazilian standards, that record would be enough to drive any manager into hiding.

Of the pressures placed upon him, Menotti says:

'People keep coming up to me and saying, 'We believe in you.' Even the government is beginning to talk about the important economical and social consequences of a World Cup victory.

'Sometimes all the responsibility frightens me. I am really scared of disappointing my people.'

The average age of Menotti's squad is 23. They are fit and strong; Menotti has worked with them for three years because he remembers only too well the shambles which preceded the 1974 World Cup, when a change of manager and tactics shortly before the finals resulted in utter chaos and confused players who were thus forced to improvise.

Perhaps the biggest threat to Menotti is his own dislike of the superstars who have gone away from Argentina. Waiting in the wings is the feared Carlos Lorenzo, the man many of the Argentinian old school would like to see in charge of the national team. Lorenzo is waiting for Menotti's home-grown young team to flop, when he could call home the 'exiles'. Lorenzo's record is akin to something out of a horror comic. He was manager of the vicious 1966 World Cup players, and the Atletico Madrid team which engaged in a bloody and disgraceful European Cup battle with Celtic at Parkhead. Wherever he has been in charge the boots have been high and the fists frighteningly free. Those with sense, and those who want Argentinian football to have some future, hope and pray that Lorenzo stays in the shadows where he belongs. If for no other reason, most of the world grudgingly wishes Luis Menotti well.

Survivors and Hopefuls

So much for the men who are safe, at least, in the knowledge that they have reached Argentina. But what of the World Cup victims – the men who have

Below: Ron Greenwood, England's highly respected team manager, who in three games in 1977 reshaped England's approach.
Facing page: Ally Macleod of Scotland, who safely steered his team to Argentina.

fallen by the wayside since 1974? Only three managers of the sixteen who led their nations to the 1974 World Cup Finals still hold their jobs: Helmut Schoen, Georg Buschner of East Germany and Georg Ericson of Sweden.

The first victim of the 1978 qualifying series was Rene Hussy of Switzerland, who was fired after his team lost to Norway in one of the biggest shock results of Group 6.

The impressive Gorski, who guided Poland into the most successful era in their soccer history, had to resign because of ill health. 'The demands on me as Poland's manager became too much to bear,' he said later.

Scotland's team manager Ally MacLeod has steered his players to a place in the finals. A flamboyant, flexible and excitable manager, his grit and determination rubbed off on his talented squad, especially in their final two matches in group seven. The 3-1 win over Czechoslovakia was a tremendous game of skill and guts; the the Czechs were stunned by the fire in the Scottish players. The last match against Wales produced a feast of exciting football from both teams but it was only toward the end that Scotland broke the deadlock with a somewhat controversial pénalty for hands. Robert Wurtz, the experienced FIFA referee, could have been wrong in his view of the incident, for photographs and television recordings seem to indicate that a Scots hand touched the ball. However, the Scots went on to hammer a second and emphatic goal to assure their place in South America.

This is the second World Cup in succession for Scotland and their dedicated supporters. Willie Ormond, their last national manager, did much in the early 1970s to improve the performance of Scottish teams, and in the 1974 tournament he led a team which had the unusual record of ending up as the only unbeaten team among the entire 16 – yet being eliminated in the first round on goal difference.

Ally MacLeod has continued the policy of developing individual skills and giving his talented players great freedom to express themselves. Skill is an important facet in a Scottish player's game; some say this comes from the fact that many players were raised in poor areas where they learned to control a ball in confined spaces against walls and on pavements! Kenny Dalglish, Danny McGrain, Don Masson,

Only three managers of the sixteen who led their nations to the 1974 World Cup Finals still hold their jobs

Martin Buchan and Lou Macari are names known in the international arena, and Ally MacLeod has in these players men that are dedicated and proud to be representing their country. Any national team manager has pressures removed immediately when he is dealing with men of skill and devotion. With these qualities MacLeod can encourage hardness and pace, although in Masson and Macari he has players who can slow the game down when necessary in midfield, and in Buchan he has an outstanding central defender. MacLeod and his squad visited South America last summer and the experience gained from a successful trip will have been immensely useful.

MacLeod will plan meticulously, and his team will play in conditions very suitable for their strength and skills. Here is a sweat merchant in an enviable position: he, and every one of his players, will be shown great respect, for Scotland's World Cup reputation is established and their results and performances over the last four years put them with the front-runners to succeed in the Argentine. Ally MacLeod must realise that gold is within his grasp – as long as his players give their usual one hundred per cent.

Elsewhere famous names are working with one aim in mind – reaching Argentina. These are men such as Holland's latest supremo, Ernst Happel, or Enzo Bearzot, who has restored the gifted Italians' self-confidence in attacking skilful football. There are many more . . . sweat merchants with their futures in someone else's hands, and feet.

If you reflect upon the driving superiority urge of the German people, the fanatical demand for continued football superiority by the success-spoiled Brazilians and the awesome undercurrent of violence, fear and resentment at being labelled 'animals' which exists in Argentina, it becomes easy to envisage the stress which the respective managers must experience when they view their prospects for 1978. Every other manager in the competition – and many, to the average fan, are anonymous – undergoes a similar ordeal. The sweat merchants are unique. They have to know every man in their charge, understand his fears, loves, strengths and weaknesses. They have to be able mentally to kick every ball for every player – yet to sit and watch while their eleven men decide whether or not tomorrow will bring continued employment.

THE CIRCUS COMES TO TOWN

The Argentine will invite two thousand million spectators from every corner of the world to watch the eleventh World Cup competition. Images from the stadiums will be transmitted via satellite for at least half an hour before each of the 38 games to the world's television screens. Buenos Aires, the World Cup city, will offer a well prepared hand to the biggest footballing circus of this century.

The object is simple; fifteen visiting nations will send their best players to compete for the top honour in football. However, the planning is tremendously complicated. It has taken eight years of slavish work by the host nation and FIFA to bring the tournament into being. From 1 June to 25 June the world will experience a tremendous sporting feast, thanks to the total dedication of a small number of men, men with a continuing vision that a gathering such as this must be one of the main contributing factors towards achieving peace amongst all men. Politics and commercialism will inevitably intervene, at times rudely, and consequently the sporting content will be somewhat tarnished, but overall it is a fact that nations are meeting nations by playing a game, and in so doing are sharing a common interest and breaking down barriers of superiority, jealousy and enmity.

Politicians will share a common interest – passionately or dispassionately according to their nature! Players will communicate through their athletic skills and spectators of all colours and creeds will share the excitement of sporting victories and defeats.

For just over three weeks the circus will be in town and will do its best to entertain.

The Work of FIFA

The Federation International de Football Association 'has the sole right to organize World Cups', and so it does every four years, each tournament creating its own particular difficulties and at times seemingly insurmountable problems. FIFA, which is nearly three-quarters of a century old, always copes and does so now in a most professional manner. It is useful to remember that FIFA is a federation which is fostering and controlling football across the world every week of every year, and the World Cup happens

Below: Argentina's President, General Jorge Rafael Videla.

Facing page top: The host nation will have passionate support from their dedicated supporters, such as this group at Buenos Aires.

Facing page below: The enormous River Plate stadium, specially rebuilt for 1978 and equipped with the very latest facilities.

to be the visible crowning glory of painstaking dedication to the game of the century.

Article 2 of the *Statutes of FIFA* (approved and adopted by Congress in 1961) reads:

The objects of the Federation are:
1. To promote the game of association football in every way which seems proper to FIFA or to its executive committee.
2. To foster friendly relations among the officials and players of national associations by encouraging football matches at all levels – amateur, non-amateur, professional – and in all other appropriate ways; . . .
4.(1) There shall be no discrimination against a country or an individual for reasons of race, religion, or politics . . .
4.(3) The national associations should prevent any racial discrimination in football, in leagues and clubs under their jurisdiction.
4.(4) In accordance with the above provisions, it is the duty of FIFA to ensure that no discrimination is practised . . .

Then further on in the Statutes is Article 39 which begins:

1. The Federation has the sole right to organize World Cups, the venue of which shall be selected by the executive committee so that these contests shall be staged successively in different continents on condition that the National Association selected is in a position to ensure that they will be organized according to the rules and financial regulations of the World Cup concerned. The World Cup cannot take place twice in succession on the same continent.
2. The team of the National Association which won the last World Cup, the team of the National Association organizing the FIFA World Cup and 14 or 18 teams of National Associations which have qualified in a preliminary competition shall participate in the final competition of the FIFA World Cup.

The Executive Committee chose the Argentine about twelve years ago for the 1978 venue, and so the host country will compete in the June finals along with West Germany, the present holders of the new golden FIFA trophy. The actual qualifying matches for the right to be amongst the final sixteen in Argentina, from a draw made in Guatemala City on 19 November 1975, got under way in 1976 and by the end of the following year the successful nations were known. The competing countries were split into the following recognised continental groupings: Africa; America (North and Central America and Caribbean); America (South); Asia; Europe; Oceania. Every competing nation has its football association affiliated to FIFA and is grouped into sensible geographically situated confederations playing within the listed continental groupings. Africa has twelve groups, America (North, Central, Caribbean) three areas, America (South) three zones, Asia four groups, Europe nine groups and Oceania one group – Asia and Oceania are

> **'... nations are meeting nations by playing a game, and in so doing are sharing a common interest and breaking down barriers of superiority, jealousy and enmity'**

linked together for the final qualifying play-offs. Looking over the complicated table of matches and results over one year of nations attempting to claim one of the coveted fourteen places in Argentina makes one realise the incredible task FIFA has as organiser, watchdog and overseer of its member nations. FIFA has in fact more member countries – 145 – than the United Nations. It is interesting to note that on achieving independence a nation generally applies for membership to FIFA first and then thinks about the value of a seat at the UN!

What is the background to organising a World Cup once the venue is designated and accepted?

After the 1966 tournament, Sir Stanley Rous and the Executive Committee considered West Germany, the Argentine, Spain, and then Bogotá, Colombia; FIFA visited the Argentine and its President to open up talks for a World Cup to be held no less than twelve years ahead. Three years before the tournament takes place a letter and application form goes out from FIFA to each National Association across the world – the application form is for nations to fill in and return should they wish to attempt to qualify for the World Cup. After the closing date for applications a meeting of FIFA's World Cup Committee, already appointed, takes place with the host nation's World Cup Committee and the grouping is decided on. Matches are organised on fixed dates and a final date is set for the qualifying matches to be completed, usually by the end of the preceding year of the finals. At last in January, when the last sixteen are announced, the 'World Cup Draw' is made, and makes banner headlines in the competing nations' newspapers. From that moment on the exciting lead-up through the media commences in earnest. For FIFA, the continuous hard work of the

Facing page: The game which assured Scotland of their place for 1978 – versus Wales at Anfield Stadium, Liverpool.
Top: Masson and Yorath lead out their teams.
Centre: Masson beats Davies from the spot for the first – and controversial – goal.
Below: Thomas heads clear as Johnstone moves in.

X FILM

→ i9A

Settle on a BRITIS...

151

'FIFA has more member countries than the United Nations'

past two years is accelerated even further: numerous meetings of finance committees have been held, press committees have taken place, technical committees have been working and the FIFA Referees' Committee have selected the final thirty-plus referees who will control the games. All the minute details of organisation will still continue to be thrashed out right up until the closing ceremony of the tournament.

The host nation, usually in the last two years, also has to accelerate its preparations tremendously, building stadiums, improving existing stadiums, preparing or building hotels and vast communication centres. Colour television via satellite must be assured, the World Cup symbols have to be finalised and commercially marketed, and arrangements across the world must be finalised for transporting thousands of 'football tourists' to the country via chosen travel agencies. The national airline must agree on specific world-wide airlines that will be permitted to fly in their guests. The attendant money-making machine is now in full swing, but on a small scale this is no bad thing, for the cost of staging the sporting circus is tremendous, and every little helps. The fees gathered from licensing World Cup trademarks and so on for commercial use are but a drop in the ocean of the host's financial planning, and even the revenue from the visiting public in the country will help very little in the end to restore any kind of immediate economic balance. Even the running costs of the three weeks of matches will outstrip the income at the turnstiles. If this seems like economic madness, we will see later in this chapter how the benefits of holding a World Cup are subtler and more complex than mere cash revenue.

FIFA has to ask, to support itself, for 10% of the gross receipts in every World Cup: it has to pay a large staff and is obliged by its statute to continue to support the amateur game and the grass roots of football – youth matches and tournaments. Because of the vast demands on FIFA, the Federation consists of: the Congress, the Supreme Governing Body, the Executive Committee and nine Standing Committees which are:

The Finance Committee
Organizing Committee for the FIFA World Cup
Amateur Committee
Referees' Committee
Players' Status Committee
Technical Committee
Medical Committee
Press and Publications Committee
Disciplinary Committee

FIFA is also by its self-made statutes teaching the underdeveloped footballing nations how to develop the domestic game and perhaps one day make progress in the fierce and established world arena. But even the 10% from World Cups and 2% from internationals, plus variable national associations' membership fees, will not permit FIFA to carry out all its invaluable work. Sponsorship from the Coca-Cola Company is now allowing the Federation to continue to carry out its work in an inflation-burdened world.

Project One is the FIFA/Coca-Cola World Football Development Programme. The idea is not new; FIFA, under the presidency of Sir Stanley Rous, worked for and achieved a great deal in this area, but now under the guidance of Dr Joao Havelange and with the aid of sponsorship a general football instruction programme has been established consisting of seminars or lectures covering administrative organisation, technique, coaching, football training, sports medicine and refereeing. Courses last six to twelve days, led by a group of four specialised intructors, addressing audiences of heads of national associations, coaches, technical directors, doctors, masseurs, referees and journalists. Government representatives and heads of sports institutions will also be invited. The four definite aims are:

1. To spread technical, administrative and scientific knowledge amongst the FIFA members.
2. To develop and promote football throughout the world, taking into account the particularities of each country.
3. To raise through this action the general standard of football, and to allow the Associations benefiting from 'Project One' to play a more and more important role in international football.
4. To realise simultaneously a wide information and promotion campaign for football at a world-wide level, in order to make this sport better known and, also, the Federation which assumes the responsibility.

FIFA decided that, in principle, all the countries of the Third World should benefit: confederations of Africa, Asia, Oceania and Concacaf, 96 associations in all. Any other national association can benefit, as they are not automatically excluded, but the priorities lie with those listed on p163.

Organising Argentina for 1978

The Argentine in 1966 was a viable proposition to host the 1978 finals, but in the intervening years economical and political disasters have hit this nation most cruelly. After the completion of the finals in West Germany a great deal of trepidation was felt about the forthcoming venue. In 1976 there was relief – in football circles at least – when the generals took over, although there could be no firm belief that they would wave a magic wand, or rather a sub-machine gun, and save a country which was almost over the brink of economic and political anarchy. As far as

Facing page top: Idol of the Scottish fans – Kenny Dalglish.
Facing page centre: The River Plate stadium, showing the new modifications made for the 1978 World Cup.
Facing page below: Davies of Wales hurls himself at the feet of Scotland striker Joe Jordan.

the sporting calendar was concerned, the country could be plunged into even more disarray, making the World Cup an impossibility. The media was full of pessimistic views and begged FIFA to switch to Brazil or even Uruguay. FIFA was unmoved, especially after their fact-finding visit in 1976, not long after Isabel Peron had been removed from making one disastrous policy after another.

General Jorge Rafael Videla headed the new government, and by the time FIFA had arrived the seeds of industrial and agricultural growth were already sown. The country was not now going to blow itself apart; the military government had arrived with definite and practical policies of piecing together a tattered land. The members of FIFA's visiting World Cup Committee were amazed at the amount of progress made in preparing for the tournament. If comparisons were to be made, the Argentine, two years before the finals were to begin, was in a more advanced state of preparation than West Germany had been at the same period. For the first time in World Cup history three new stadiums – at Mendoza, Cordoba and Mar Del Plata – were being built and another three – Velez Sarsfield, Rosario Central and the River Plate – substantially remodelled. They will be fine and lasting stadiums, housing gymnasiums, spacious dressing and first aid rooms, basketball courts and various other facilities for future generations of Argentinians to enjoy. The playing surfaces are being relaid and will have ample time to settle. The River Plate in the north of Buenos Aires will be the main stadium for the tournament. It was built for the 1951 Pan-American games, and by 1978 will hold

82,000 spectators, desks for 1200 journalists, 40 radio and TV cabins, telex and photocopying machines, post offices, cafeterias, restaurants, press conference rooms, filming and recording labs, all readily available for the media people.

A considerable worry for FIFA was the communications set-up. Would a sophisticated global audience actually see the 1978 finals in colour from their armchairs? What FIFA saw immediately allayed these fears. Enormous strides were being taken to supply the world with the sporting excitement as it happens – microwave emission through an artificial satellite will supply all needs for telephone and cable communications simultaneously, process data at high speed and transmit and receive television in colour.

The other priority on FIFA's list was security, especially as this was and still is a nation at war with guerilla activity. The media was expressing great concern for all the national associations that hoped their teams would reach the opening ceremony in the River Plate Stadium. Once again surprise and relief was felt at the tightness of security arrangements. Security seemed to hover quietly in the background, firmly and surely suppressing any danger.

FIFA returned to Zurich and announced to the

Below: A prize for every contestant – Sir Stanley Rous (centre) with youth trophies in Mexico in 1970.

Facing page top: Rous arrives in Santiago in 1962 to be met by Chile's vice-president of the FIFA organising committee, del Pena.

Facing page centre: Studying plans for Aztec stadium.

Facing page below: Rous is presented to the Pope as the European representative of EUFA.

EAM, the Argentine organising body of the World Cup, is government-run and stands for *Emte Autár Quico Mundial*. Its president is a retired general, Antonio Luis Merlo, who is an excellent public-relations figure. With him is the hard-working vice-president, Captain Carlos Alberto Lacoste, a forceful and dominant figure who is pushing the whole programme through at a breakneck speed.

The Argentine will be ready in good time, and the facilities overall will be first class – yet why does a nation ever want to host this huge sporting occasion, especially when the cost and immediate return is considered? There are three answers. The first is the simple and straightforward honour of holding the World Cup finals. Secondly, in doing so a country speeds up many development plans that otherwise could be shelved for years, such as building amenities to expand the tourist trade, constructing and improving stadiums for the use of increasing leisure time, and seizing the chance to develop communications, for an event such as the World Cup will bequeath a dense intercommunication network which, were it not for this event, would normally go through a tedious and slow development. Thirdly, it is a unique public relations opportunity for making known a country's philosophy, history and traditions, its capacity for producing, its cultural richness and even a glimpse of its future. 1978 will put Argentina very firmly on the map.

The Argentine, with its 25,000,000 inhabitants spread across a land of varying beauties and differing landscapes, from frozen Atlantic continent to lush green mountain ranges, majestic and lovely lakes to the overcrowded cosmopolitan capital, is waiting impatiently to receive the fifteen nations competing with them for the coveted trophy. Argentinians love their football as much or more than their food! This says something, for Buenos Aires has such a wide variety of gourmet food available that the capital is placed amongst the top ten gastronomic cities of the world!

When thinking about there edible delights, consider also the arriving national teams and the care and attention that has to be taken over their food and diets. There must be no chance whatsoever of tummy troubles or food poisoning; no 'foreign food' can be permitted to put at risk players' stamina and mental approach to a match. Enormous expense is lavished on flying over doctors and chefs and home-produced food for the teams. Doctors monitor and plan the daily food intake and top-class chefs prepare the food exactly as it is required. The only 'wobbly' tummies around will be caused by pre-match nerves and nothing else!

The Playing Equipment

When these players walk out into the stadium for each match they will be wearing specially designed strips (shirts, shorts and stockings) and boots which

Top: Adi Dassler in pre-war days in his old factory, showing the antiquated equipment on which his sporting equipment was then produced – a contrast with the picture overleaf.
Left: Dassler explains the subtleties of his latest lightweight football shoe to Franz Beckenbauer.

are carefully designed to suit their needs and comfort and to act as aids to their considerable skills. They will also be playing with a specially designed football that will never hinder the flow of play. So another specialist joins the ranks of doctors and chefs – a man named Adi Dassler. This single man has revolutionised the football boot and produced a ball which is ahead of all its rivals.

More than half a century ago he was producing quality shoes in Germany on what to the modern eye looks like antique machinery. His shoes were first-class and much care and attention was put into each pair. This was a craft that Dassler was proud of, as only the best could come from his workshop. Soon the man's thoughts were directed to sporting foot-wear, for he felt the athlete's feet deserved just as much care and attention and suitable gear would no doubt help him compete in comfort. For nearly half a century his company Adidas – with the famous clover-leaf trademark and the three lines on each boot – have been supplying sportsmen of the world with the best footwear. A museum in Hertzo-genaurach, Germany, shows the history of dedica-tion and development in this man's work and the significance of his own and the company's help to athletes the world over. Adidas is the largest sports shoe manufacturer in the world and through advanced technology they produce truly high performance equipment.

Today's generation of football players must be amazed that their forefathers – right up until the 1950s – were wearing clumsy 'armoured boots' weighing over 500 grammes. These and earlier boots, weighing an astonishing 600 grammes, were lugged

Clockwise from top right: Latest developments in shinpads; the new boot designed for artificial playing surfaces; the Adidas museum; electronic equipment for testing new football shoe designs; the development of the football boot within two decades – shedding 300 grammes per boot in the process.

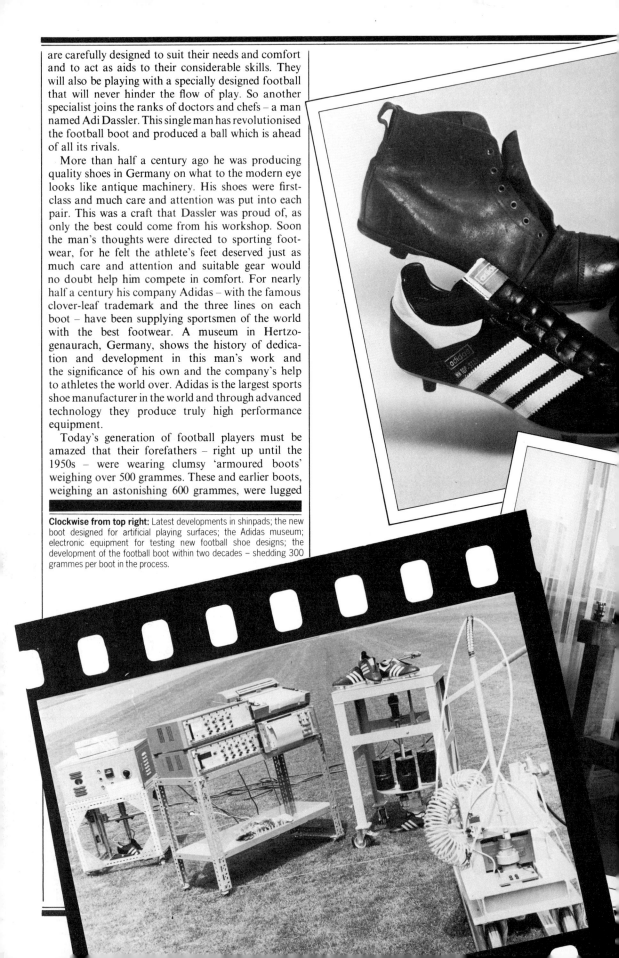

around by players used to kicking the ball with the toe. A steel cap was therefore inserted to protect the toes! The Germans in the 1950s gave some logical thought to the design of boots and the advantages of lighter footwear at a time when attitudes to and techniques of ball control were changing; more sensitive control using the instep was being practised and used. Just imagine the weights players had been dragging around with them for so many years. If the weight of a boot is reduced by 100 grammes, a pair can be made 200 grammes lighter. When this weight difference is multiplied by the approximately ten thousand steps a football player takes during a normal game then there is a total weight reduction of two metric tons! From the mid-1950s until today huge advances have been made, and in the forefront has been Adi Dassler, the shoemaker with a love of sport. His real fame began in 1953 with the introduction of football boots with interchangeable cleats (studs). More than fifty improvements in cleats and cleat styles have developed since then. Since 1953 Adidas have continued to pioneer increasingly lightweight – yet super strong – footwear which we would now call football *shoes*. From the gigantic boot of 1895 weighing a massive 20·6 ounces, the present shoe now weighs in at 8·5 ounces, and supplies equal protection. The modern shoe is nothing more than a second skin for the foot, with which the ball is not so much kicked, but to a great extent 'guided'. There are many models, some specifically designed for injury-prone football legs or those with a certain weakness, others for synthetic turf or as an aid to special skills.

'The ball is round!' This oft-quoted phrase coined by senior West German trainer Sepp Herberger is not strictly true, for the ball does lose its shape in every football game. The ball is not always really round when struck with force with the instep, head or the fist of the goalkeeper. When the ball receives a severe blow it can be compressed to as much as 40% of its volume; therefore the ball has to be built to take a beating, for it is kicked, passed, dribbled and shot hundreds of times per game. A good instep drive can propel a ball at 100 kilometres per hour. All that can be said for the balls produced at the turn of the century is that they were *relatively* round. The ball supplied by Adidas for the 1978 World Cup is made from 32 cowhide sections, which are assembled to form the ball's spherical shape from twenty white hectagons and twelve black pentagons; black and white was originally conceived for black and white television reception, and is now accepted as the traditional international ball. It is hand-sewn with wear-and-tear-resistant nylon and then covered with a polyurethane coating to make it waterproof. This coating ensures that the ball even when soaking wet will not weigh more than 453 grammes. When dry, it is not permitted to be less than 396 grammes in weight.

Argentinian Football

The early influence of the English remains in the Argentine with clubs such as the River Plate, Newell's Old Boys and Rosario Central – a relic of the once British-owned railways. The British settled in and around Buenos Aires, sharing the capital with an equally large number of Spaniards. The area became

> **Football boots in 1895 weighed over twenty ounces—now they weigh less than seven**

immensely rich, with the British owning and running banks and railways. It is believed that this country held the largest British community outside the Commonwealth and Argentina soon became a European-type country in South America. Eventually the number of British inhabitants decreased but the game of football that they had introduced continued its huge popularity. Since the early 1930s the main league competition, the Metropolitan First Division, has been in operation, followed by the National Championship which is now about ten years old. Provincial clubs who are not in the Metropolitan League are able to qualify for the championship. In 1977, 23 clubs played 44 matches in the Metropolitan, which usually starts around February and carries through until November. Boca Juniors won both the competitions in 1976 and would seem to be going from strength to strength. In the South American Cup – the equivalent of the European Cup – River Plate were runners-up. In this competition Argentina holds an excellent record: Independiente were four times winners previously and Argentinian teams have reached the final on fourteen consecutive occasions.

As far as the national team is concerned there is much positive hope generating across Argentina. In 1976 only Brazil had a better record in South America than the Argentinians. They played thirteen matches, won eight, drew two and lost three. Two of these three defeats came in the Atlantic Cup and were inflicted by Brazil at home and away. This competition saw Argentina come second after defeating both Uruguay and Paraguay twice. Later in the year the national team beat Peru 3-1 (away), Chile 2-0 (home) and drew 0-0 at home to Russia. In February 1977 they beat Hungary 5-1 at the Boca Juniors Stadium in Buenos Aires. In March the national players were packed off to Real Madrid's 75th anniversary tournament, beating Iran on penalty-kicks in the semi-final before losing the final 1-0 to Real. 'Friendlies' during 1977 saw them match themselves against top visiting national teams and they only lost against West Germany, 1-3, gaining useful wins against Poland 3-1, Yugoslavia 1-0 and East Germany 2-0. Draws were achieved against England, Scotland

Top: The official logo for the 1978 World Cup.
Centre: Street scene in downtown Buenos Aires.
Below: FIFA's President Dr. Jaoa Havelange. Argentina will be the first World Cup held under his tutelage. He would be the first to acknowledge and to continue in his own way Rous's ideals.

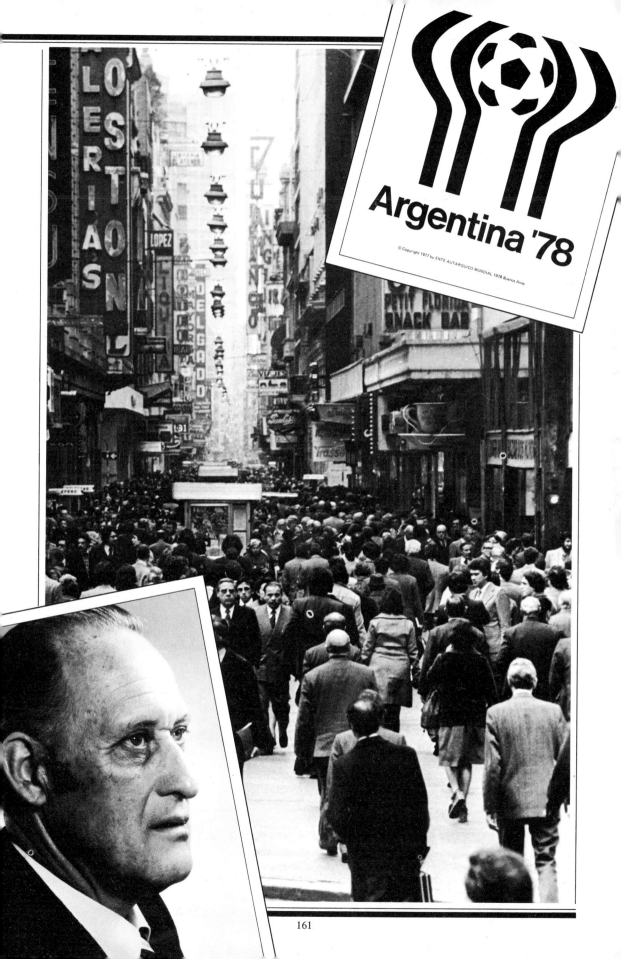

Argentina '78

© Copyright 1977 by ENTE AUTARQUICO MUNDIAL 1978 Buenos Aires

and France.

Cesar Luis Menotti, a young man of 37, was appointed team manager in September 1974. He had made a fine reputation for himself as a coach in charge of Huracan in 1973, when he led them to the first division championship. At the moment he is one of a rare breed, having managed to last nearly four years in sole charge of a national team! This is probably not too surprising, for the public are pleased to see that he has retained in the national team the same attractive style of play he became famous for at Huracan, despite the fact that most Argentinian sides now play the harder and more physical game – the very manner in which Boca Juniors are playing with great success. However, Menotti will stick to the principle of encouraging his players to play attractive attacking football; this can only do good for the Argentinian game, for over the years – from the painful scenes in the 1966 World Cup – their style of play has not been looked upon very favourably. Now that Argentina are the hosts it is imperative that a good and sporting image be shown to the world, without losing their grit and determination to win. The young Menotti would seem the ideal choice to shape the national team into a unit that can approach each match in the tournament in this manner. One of the main problems facing Menotti is that many of his best players have gone abroad, particularly to Spain, in the last few years. In fact only Rene Houseman and Jorge Carrascosa remain in the current squad from the 1974 World Cup. Probably the best of the exiles is Mario Kempes, and increasing pressure is being put on Menotti to bring back this free-scoring star for the finals.

It is fair to say that over the last two years Menotti has achieved a considerable amount with his squad. There may be no apparent stars – never mind super-stars – to catch the eye at the moment, but who knows what could be coaxed from a number of highly talented and fresh young players? The major problem which Menotti must help his players overcome is the slow build-up in attack. Against European teams they find they have less time to stay on the ball, stroking it about in a measured fashion as in their domestic football, and this at times tends to throw them out of their stride. It is a certainty that Menotti will be working hard on this.

It is also a certainty that the team will receive fanatical support in the packed stadiums – as usual, mass emotion will be willing the host team to World Cup glory. In return this will put enormous pressure on the players, but if when the whistle blows to start each match the players can shrug off their tension and enjoy the support pushing them on, who knows what could be achieved? Argentina must be more than a dark horse for the 1978 final.

Football is a Universal Language

Dr Joao Havelange coined this phrase to sum up his attitude to the international game and what it should mean to all national Associations, their players and loyal supporters. This will be Havelange's first World Cup as president of FIFA and one which he would like to be memorably successful. There is no reason why this desire should not be granted, and it is a wish that is echoed by millions across the globe.

This quote from Dr Havelange comes from the magazine *FIFA News*, just after he was voted President in 1974:

'I think it is a happy coincidence that the ball is the instrument of the sport represented by FIFA. It is round, without angles or sharp edges. With its unlimited surface, lines may criss-cross to infinity. When in motion, it can be impelled in all directions with no deformation and without losing its charac- teristics. To fulfill its performance, however, it is necessary for it to be always on the move, never still. I feel that I can take the ball as the symbol of my administration in the presidency of FIFA. With the good co-operation and help of all affiliated nations, FIFA will certainly be in perpetual motion all over the world, bringing an important contribution to the coming together and understanding among nations, as a decisive participation of sport towards peace among men.'

When the opening ceremony takes place in the River Plate Stadium on 1 June 1978, the emotive implications of Dr Havelange's words will be experienced by all the people present in the stadium or watching on television screens. FIFA will have brought about the eleventh World Cup in a time of increasing global unrest and in a country that only FIFA originally had faith in for such a sporting enterprise. In March 1977 the *New York Times* said:

'Gratuitous criminal violence occurs in Buenos Aires with a frequency insignificant compared to New York or other large American cities. For the tourist, then, Argentina is about as safe as any place in the world and safer than many.'

In the same month a piece in the *Economist* read:

'Only a year away from virtual economic collapse, Argentinians have recovered enough to demand instant prosperity. A year ago people were saying that they would be satisfied with survival; now the popular chorus in the football stadiums is "bring back the thieves!"'

The 1978 World Cup will be a celebration of the world's favourite team game and a celebration for the Argentine and its people. Two years ago black clouds started to lift from this suffering country, and now the sun can shine on its swift recovery. They will happily and proudly welcome the world, for they want to share their economic and cultural revival and most of all their enthusiasm for World Cup football.

As Pele remarked on his retirement:

'After all these years in soccer, I have come to realise that through soccer, we can become brothers. Football's appeal and magnitude is such that it ignores race, religion and politics. Soccer has one real goal and that is to create friendship.'

Fédération Internationale de Football Association

PROJECT 1 DEVELOPMENT AND PROMOTION PROGRAMME
GLOBAL RECAPITULATION AND DETAILED INVENTORY

CONTINENTS	TOTAL	ENGLISH	FRENCH	SPANISH
Africa	36	17	19	—
Asia	34	29	5	—
Oceania	4	4	—	—
Concacaf	22	11	1	10
	96	61	25	10

*without South Africa and Rhodesia

AFRICA	ASIA	OCEANIA	CONCACAF
Algeria	Afghanistan	Australia	Antigua
Burundi	Bahrain	Fiji	Bahamas
Cameroon	Bangladesh	New Zealand	Barbados
Central Africa	Brunei	Papua-New Guinea	Bermuda
Congo	Burma		Canada
Dahomey	China Nat.		Costa Rica
Egypt AR	Hong Kong		Cuba
Ethiopia	India		Domin. Republic
Gabon	Indonesia		Guatemala
Gambia	Iran		Guyana
Ghana	Iraq		Haiti
Guinea	Israel		Honduras
Ivory Coast	Japan		Jamaica
Kenya	Jordan		Mexico
Lesotho	Khmer		Neth. Antilles
Liberia	Korea DPR		Nicaragua
Libya	Korea Rep.		Panama
Madagascar	Kuwait		Puerto Rico
Malawi	Laos		El Salvador
Mali	Lebanon		Surinam
Mauritania	Malaysia		Trinidad
Mauritius	Nepal		USA
Morocco	Pakistan		
Niger	Philippines		
Nigeria	Qatar		
Senegal	Saudi Arabia		
Sierra Leone	Singapore		
Somalia	Sri Lanka		
Sudan	Syria		
Tanzania	Thailand		
Togo	United Arab Emirates		
Tunisia	Vietnam DPR		
Uganda	Vietnam Rep.		
Upper Volta	Yemen DPR		
Zaire			
Zambia			

APPENDIX: THE ROAD TO ARGENTINA

THE 16 QUALIFYING COUNTRIES FOR THE 1978 WORLD CUP

The countries in capitals represent qualifying teams.

1 ARGENTINA   The host country.
2 W. GERMANY   The present World Champions.

FINAL GROUP TABLES FOR QUALIFYING MATCHES

	P	W	D	L	F	A	Pts.
3 POLAND	6	5	1	0	17	4	11
Portugal	6	4	1	1	12	7	9
Denmark	6	2	0	4	14	12	4
Cyprus	6	0	0	6	4	24	0
4 ITALY	6	5	0	1	18	4	10
England	6	5	0	1	15	4	10
Finland	6	2	0	4	11	16	4
Luxemburg	6	0	0	6	2	22	0
5 AUSTRIA	6	4	2	0	14	2	10
East Germany	6	3	3	0	15	4	9
Turkey	6	2	1	3	9	5	5
Malta	6	0	0	6	0	27	0
6 HOLLAND	6	5	1	0	11	3	11
Belgium	6	3	0	3	7	6	6
N. Ireland	6	2	1	3	7	6	5
Iceland	6	1	0	5	2	12	2
7 FRANCE	4	2	1	1	7	4	5
Bulgaria	4	1	2	1	5	6	4
Rep. of Ireland	4	1	1	2	2	4	3
8 SWEDEN	4	3	0	1	7	4	6
Norway	4	2	0	2	3	4	4
Switzerland	4	1	0	3	3	5	2
9 SCOTLAND	4	3	0	1	6	3	6
Czechoslavakia	4	2	0	2	4	6	4
Wales	4	1	0	3	3	4	2
10 SPAIN	4	3	0	1	4	1	6
Rumania	4	2	0	2	7	8	4
Yugoslavia	4	1	0	3	6	7	2

	P	W	D	L	F	A	Pts.
11 HUNGARY	4	2	1	1	6	4	5
Russia	4	2	0	2	5	3	4
Greece	4	1	1	2	2	6	3

Hungary met Bolivia, losers of the South American play-off, for a place in the finals.

Hungary 6 Bolivia   0
Bolivia   2 Hungary 3

SOUTH AMERICA

		P	W	D	L	F	A	Pts.
G1	BRAZIL	4	2	2	0	8	1	6
	Paraguay	4	1	2	1	3	3	4
	Columbia	4	0	2	2	1	8	2
G2	BOLIVIA	4	3	1	0	8	3	7
	Uruguay	4	1	2	1	5	4	4
	Venezuela	4	0	1	3	2	8	1
G3	PERU	4	2	2	0	8	2	6
	Chile	4	2	1	1	5	3	5
	Ecuador	4	0	1	3	1	9	1

Brazil, Bolivia and Peru won their way to a play-off for two places in Argentina.

SOUTH AMERICAN PLAY-OFF

	P	W	D	L	F	A	Pts.
12 BRAZIL	2	2	0	0	9	0	4
13 PERU	2	1	0	1	5	1	2
Bolivia	2	0	0	2	0	13	0

AFRICA

	P	W	D	L	F	A	Pts.
14 TUNISIA	4	2	0	1	7	4	5
Egypt	4	2	1	2	7	11	4
Nigeria	4	1	1	2	5	4	3

ASIA

	P	W	D	L	F	A	Pts.
15 IRAN	8	6	2	0	12	3	14
Korea Republic	8	3	4	1	12	8	10
Kuwait	8	4	1	3	13	8	9
Australia	8	3	1	4	11	8	7
Hong Kong	8	0	0	8	5	26	0

CONCACAF

	P	W	D	L	F	A	Pts.
16 MEXICO	4	4	0	0	20	0	10
Haiti	5	3	1	1	6	6	7
El Salvador	5	2	1	2	8	9	5
Canada	5	2	1	2	7	8	5
Guatemala	5	1	1	3	8	10	3
Surinam	5	0	0	5	6	17	0

THE DRAW FOR THE 1978 WORLD CUP FINAL ROUNDS

The draw, made in Buenos Aires on 14 January 1978, was made as follows.

There are four containers, each bearing names of four countries. Each group is made up by removing one country from each container. Countries to be kept apart in the first round are placed in the same container.

FIFA regulations state that the cup holders (West Germany) and the host country (Argentina) will be seeded in different groups. As for the rest, the seeding will follow similar geographical lines to those followed in 1974.

The draw was:
Cup 1 – Brazil, Argentina, Chile, Uruguay.
Cup 2 – W. Germany, Italy, Netherlands, Scotland.
Cup 3 – Bulgaria, East Germany, Poland, Yugoslavia.
Cup 4 – Australia, Zaire, Haiti, Sweden.

To decide the four semi-finalists, the tournament will be played in two rounds:

ROUND 1

16 teams will be divided into 4 groups of 4 teams each. The division of these teams into groups is made by the organising committee in public by means of seeding and a draw having regard to the geographical position of the countries represented.

Group 1 – Numbers 1, 2, 3, 4.
Group 2 – Numbers 5, 6, 7, 8.
Group 3 – Numbers 9, 10, 11, 12.
Group 4 – Numbers 13, 14, 15, 16.

The system of play is a league system (addition of points). Each team plays one match against each of the other teams in the same group, with two points for a win, one point for a draw and no points for a defeat. The two leading teams of each group will qualify for **Round Two.**

To prevent teams who have already played together in Round One from meeting again in Round Two, the eight teams will form two groups as follows:

GROUP A	GROUP B
1st team Group I – No A1	2nd team Group I – No B5
2nd team Group II – No A2	1st team Group II – No B6
1st team Group III – No A3	2nd team Group III – No B7
2nd team Group IV – No A4	1st team Group IV – No B8

These groups will be decided as in Round One.

The second team in each group will play for 3rd and 4th place and the leading team of each group will qualify for the final.

The draw for formation of groups was made according to the decisions to be taken by the FIFA World Cup Organising Committee on 12 January 1978 in Buenos Aires. It was held on 14 January 1978, at 8.00 local time at the TEATRO SAN MARTIN, B.A.

Three-year-old Ricardo Teixeira Havelange, grandson of FIFA President Dr. Joâo Havelange, stood on the huge table and with great confidence took the names of the qualified countries out of the various cups.

THE FOUR GROUPS IN ROUND ONE

Group 1 – To be played in Buenos Aires and Mar de Plata.

	P	W	D	L	F	A	Pts.
1 ARGENTINA*							
2 HUNGARY							
3 FRANCE							
4 ITALY							

Group 2 – To be played in Buenos Aires, Cordoba and Rosario.

5 POLAND							
6 W. GERMANY*							
7 TUNISIA							
8 MEXICO							

Group 3 – To be played in Buenos Aires and Mar de Plata.

9 AUSTRIA							
10 SPAIN							
11 SWEDEN							
12 BRAZIL*							

Group 4 – To be played in Cordoba and Mendoza.

13 HOLLAND*							
14 PERU							
15 IRAN							
16 SCOTLAND							

*Seeded by FIFA before the Draw.
Italy were placed in the first group, though not officially seeded.

Round Two: To be played in Buenos Aires, Rosario, Cordoba and Mendoza.

Group A

Group B

Play-off for 3rd and 4th place, 24 June 1978:

v

World Cup Final, 25 June 1978:

v

World Cup Champions 1978:

MATCH TIMETABLE – FINAL COMPETITION

		Group 1		Group 2			Group 3		Group 4	
		Buenos Aires	Mar del Plata	Buenos Aires	Rosario	Cordoba	Buenos Aires	Mar del Plata	Cordoba	Mendoza
Round one	1 June				6:5					
	2 June	2:1	3:4		7:8					
	3 June						10:9	11:12	15:16	14:13
	6 June	1:3	4:2		5:7	8:6				
	7 June						9:11	12:10	16:14	13:15
	10 June	4:1	3:2		8:5	7:6				
	11 June						11:10	12:9	15:14	16:13
Round Two	14 June	A2:A1		B6:B5		A3:A4				B7:B8
	18 June	A1:A3		B5:B7		A4:A2				B8:B6
	21 June	A4:A1		B8:B5		A3:A2				B7:B6
3rd and 4th Place Final	24 June									
World Cup Final	25 June									

FOOTNOTES ON THE 1978 WORLD CUP FINALS

Football pundits the world over feel that the World Cup champions will emerge from the four favourites: Brazil, West Germany, Argentina and Holland. Scotland and Italy are the fancied outsiders. The 1978 finals could be immensely exciting for who knows what France, Austria, Hungary, Mexico and Spain will produce in the first week? There is every chance that we shall see talent in depth spread throughout the four groups. FIFA have, with sensible seeding and luck in the draw, produced four exciting groups and the world audience could be watching a World Cup to be remembered for its all round skill and attacking football. Here are the authors' opinions of the competing teams:

SCOTLAND	bubbling over with talent and confidence.
FRANCE	with their best team for years.
SPAIN	battling along with increasing belief in themselves.
SWEDEN	a little country and there again on merit.
AUSTRIA	a determined hard-working team.
POLAND	full of experience and with many of their 1974 players.
HUNGARY	given the chance, a goal-scoring machine.
PERU	youth is not on their side but they have patience and talent.
ARGENTINA	if they can keep their heads and play football they could be very hard to beat.
HOLLAND	even without Cruyff they have the talent to reach the final again.
BRAZIL	cannot be discounted when playing on South American soil.
W. GERMANY	controlled by the legendary Schoen, they will work their talent to the full.
ITALY	if they play honestly and are not homesick they will please themselves and the vast audience.
IRAN	they will impress with skill and fitness.
TUNISIA	although lacking experience as a team in the World Cup arena individual flair will show.

Picture Credits

Adidas: 156–7, 158–9

Conrad Film Associates: 3 (right), 5 (left), 69, 74 (below left), 93 (centre), 94, 95, 111, 114–5, 116–7, 118–9, 120–1, 122 (top and below), 124–5, 126–7, 131, 133, 135 (left), 139 (below right), 140 (top), 142 (top), 144–5, 149 (below), 151, 152 (centre)

FIFA: 1 (below), 23, 24 (right), 25 (below), 26–7, 28, 30–1, 44, 50, 54 (below), 161

Football Association: 14 (below), 16, 17, 18, 19, 33, 53
Frank O'Farrell: 112

Popperfoto: 1 (top), 2, 10, 24 (left), 29, 32, 34–5, 36–7, 38, 40 (top), 41 (below), 42–3, 47, 51, 54 (top), 55, 58 (top), 63, 66–7, 70–1, 76 (below), 80, 82–3, 102 (top), 105, 128–9 (below), 132, 134, 136 (below), 138 (left), 140 (below), 144 (top), 163

Press Association: 4 (left), 39 (top), 40 (below), 41 (top), 57, 65, 96, 98, 101 (far right), 146

Radio Times Hulton Picture Library: 12–13, 14 (top), 15, 18–19, 20–1, 25 (top)

Peter Robinson: 3 (left), 4 (right), 5 (right), 6, 9, 46, 48, 58 (below), 60, 64, 72, 74 (top and below right), 76 (top), 77, 78 (right), 81 (below), 91, 92, 93, 97, 103, 109, 110, 128–9 (top), 130, 135 (top and below), 138 (right), 139 (top and below left), 141, 142 (below), 147, 151, 152 (top and below)

Sir Stanley Rous: 81 (left), 84–5, 90, 106, 107 (below), 122 (centre), 154–5

Saxon and Lindströms: 136 (top)

Jack Taylor: 99, 107 (above), 100–1

Western Mail: 102 (below right)

Based on the international television series created by
Derek Conrad and Robert Sidaway.

A Conrad Film Associates International Ltd/Polytel Film
Ltd production.